Contents

Feminism, Identity and Difference

First published in 1999 in Great Britain by
FRANK CASS PUBLISHERS
Newbury House, 900 Eastern Avenue,
Ilford, Essex IG2 7HH

and in the United States of America by
FRANK CASS PUBLISHERS
c/o ISBS
5804 N.E. Hassalo Street
Portland, Oregon 97213-3644

Website: www.frankcass.com

British Library Cataloguing in Publication Data

Feminism, identity and difference
1. Feminism 2. Gender identity
I. Hekman, Susan J.
305.4`1
ISBN 0 7146 5017 X

ISBN 0 7146 5017 X (cloth)
ISBN 0 7146 8074 5 (paper)

Library of Congress Cataloging in Publication Data

Feminism, identity, and difference / edited by Susan Hekman.
p. cm.
Includes bibliographical references and index.
ISBN 0-7146-5017-X (alk. paper). -- ISBN 0-7146-8074-5 (pbk. : alk. paper)
1. Feminism. 2. Feminity. 3. Feminist theory. 4. Women--Identity. I. Hekman, Susan J.
HQ1150.F454 1999
305.43--dc21 99-31186
CIP

This group of studies first appeared in a Special Issue on 'Feminism, Identity and Difference' of CRISPP 2/1 (Spring 1999) ISSN 1369-8230
Published by Frank Cass

Printed in Great Britain by Antony Rowe Ltd., Chippenham, Wilts.

Introduction

This special issue of CRISPP focuses on a set of issues that are at the forefront of feminist thought in the late 1990s: identity, difference, and their implications for feminist politics. As feminism moves into an era in which differences among women, the multiple identities of women, and identity politics are at the centre of feminist discussions, new approaches, methods, and politics are called for. 'Woman' as a universal identity that informs feminist theory and practice is no longer a viable basis for feminism. Yet precisely what can replace 'woman' is still unclear. Multiple identities and differences solve some of the questions entailed by 'woman', yet raise others. The papers in this volume represent attempts to sort through some of these problems and suggest solutions.

My contribution, 'Identity Crises: Identity, Identity Politics, and Beyond', offers an overview of the problems created by the contemporary feminist focus on identity and difference. I argue that although the question of identity is central to feminism, identity politics has created a set of contradictions for feminist theory and practice that are intractable. I advance two theses. First, feminists must develop a theory of the social construction of identity specifically tailored to feminist purposes. Second, feminists must move beyond identity politics. Bringing the issue of identity into feminist or any other politics has resulted in the reification of identity. Against the proponents of identity politics, I argue that feminism should eschew identity in the political arena because it harks back to the politics of liberalism/modernism.

Nancy Hirschmann's article, 'Difference as an Occasion for Rights', is an attempt to do what many feminists have claimed is impossible: reconcile feminism and liberalism. In a highly nuanced argument,

Hirschmann contends that liberalism is a diverse ideology, offering multiple possibilities for the definition and redefinition of its central concepts. Specifically, she argues that one of liberalism's central concepts, rights, can be redefined to allow for the kind of group rights that feminism requires. Liberalism, she claims, is the framework in which political battles are carried out; it does not pre-determine the result. Hirschmann's conclusion is that redefining rights through care provides for a 'concrete universality' that reflects feminist values.

Shane Phelan's 'Bodies, Passions, and Citizenship' is much less sanguine about the possibility of integrating American political ideology with the 'others' (including women) that it has marginalised. Focusing on the conception of the body and the body politic in American Republican thought, Phelan argues that this body is not just male, but masculinist and the bearer of what she calls phallic agency. For this body politic, any deviation from the 'generic' category is a threat. The task for these others, she argues, is to find ways of penetrating this phallic masculinity. The strategy she advocates is devising 'micro-challenges' to that concept by placing pressure at weak points in the edifice.

Eloise Buker assumes, with Phelan, that liberalism must be displaced rather than redefined. But for Buker, the tools are already at hand. Her thesis is that the emerging postmodern self is very similar to the feminine self as it has been defined in the modern political tradition. Buker's task is to demonstrate that this postmodern self is a responsible, ethical citizen, despite its fragmentation and fuzzy boundaries. She accomplishes this by detailing the ethical implications of the postmodern self. This self, embodied most clearly in the modern female, brings care, responsibility, and relatedness to the political arena, forging a new conception of the citizen for the postmodern world.

Rajani Sudan's 'Feminising Race' examines the question of identity and its re-articulation from a radically different perspective. Questioning whether the re-articulation of identity originates in the abstract theorising of academics, Sudan suggests that we look instead to popular culture. Her insightful analysis of the popular film Disclosure suggests that the contemporary re-articulation of identities of race and gender are a product of our new understanding of the ontology of labour. In the global marketplace, the 'foreign' and the 'exotic' are displaced and conflated with the feminine.

SUSAN HEKMAN
University of Texas at Arlington

1

Identity Crises: Identity, Identity Politics, and Beyond

SUSAN HEKMAN

In 1988, *Signs* published an article by Linda Alcoff, 'Cultural Feminism Versus Post-structuralism: the Identity Crisis in Feminist Theory'. In her article, Alcoff addresses the crisis in feminist theory that dominated feminist thought in the late 1980s: the conflict between 'cultural feminism' and post-structuralism. This dispute revolved around the definition of 'woman' in feminist theory and practice. The cultural feminists argued for an essentialist definition of woman, the post-structuralists rejected the possibility of any definition. Alcoff attempts to define a compromise between these two extremes, arguing for a concept of the subject as a dialectical interaction between the inner world of subjectivity and the outer world of social forces.

Alcoff's article has become an important touchstone in the debate over the concept of 'woman' that has occupied feminist theory in the 1980s and 1990s. At stake in this debate is nothing less than the definition of a new paradigm for knowledge and subjectivity, a paradigm that displaces the masculinist assumptions of modernist thought. Alcoff's reference to 'identity crisis' in the title of her article indicates the importance of the issue for feminist theory. In the course of her article, however, Alcoff briefly discusses another sense of 'identity' that, in the late 1980s, was coming to the forefront in feminist theory and practice: identity politics. She defines identity politics as taking one's identity as a political point of departure, a motivation for action and a delineation of one's politics (Alcoff, 1988, pp.431–2). Alcoff argues that although identity is a necessary point of departure for the subject, it must always be conceived as a construction, not a fixed entity. She thus argues that identity politics is an offshoot of the post-structuralist rejection of a fixed, essential identity. Identity politics, she concludes, has the effect of problematising the connection between identity and politics (Alcoff, 1988, pp.432–3).

I begin this discussion of identity and identity politics in feminist theory and practice with Alcoff's article for two reasons. First, it illustrates how, in the subsequent decade, the focus of feminist theory has shifted. For Alcoff, the 'crisis' in feminist theory was not about identity. Identity politics was a subsidiary issue; the real issue was defining a new paradigm for feminism. In the 1990s, however, the issues raised by identity politics have created a different crisis in feminist theory, a crisis that is specifically about the connection between identity and politics. This crisis has derailed feminist theory from the debate that Alcoff discusses, confounding its key issues. This new 'identity crisis' raises issues that are crucial to the evolution of feminism, yet seem, at least at this point, intractable.

My second reason for beginning with Alcoff is that her article provides an early illustration of the most confounding aspect of the debate over identity and identity politics: the disjunction between theory and practice. Alcoff, along with subsequent theorists of identity politics, defines it as compatible with the post-structuralist rejection of identity. This definition has not proved accurate. In practice, identity politics has not, as many theorists have argued, problematised the connection between identity and politics, but, rather, made embracing a specific, fixed identity a precondition for political action. The emphasis on the differences among women now dominating feminism should have had the effect of problematising identity itself, revealing the constructedness and fluidity of identity. But the practice of identity politics has not realised this potential. Women claiming a political identity as African-American women, Asian women, Chicanas, and so on do not enter the political arena asserting those identities as provisional and constructed, but, rather, as fixed and true. Identity politics is not about identities as fictions, but identities as truth.

My intention in the following is to provide an overview of the issues raised by identity politics and, thus, to substantiate the argument that identity politics has led feminism into a morass of confusions and contradictions. It is imperative that feminists get on with the task of defining a new paradigm of knowledge and subjectivity, a task that identity politics has hindered rather than advanced. My goal is not so much to offer a solution to the crisis created by identity politics, but to move beyond the dilemmas it has created – to a feminist politics without identity.

Identity and Difference

One of the central tenets of deconstruction, if, indeed, deconstruction can be said to have tenets at all, is that opposites inhabit each other. There is no better illustration of this thesis than the concept of identity. Identity is necessarily defined by two opposites: sameness and difference. To declare that something or someone has a particular identity is to claim, simultaneously, that it is identical to the other entities that possess that identity and that, as a particular thing, it possesses unique qualities, that is, an identity. Perhaps more than any other concept, 'identity' is defined by this play of opposites.

The OED separates these opposites into two distinct definitions of identity: '1. The quality of being the same in substance, composition, nature, properties, or in particular qualities under consideration; absolute or essential sameness... 2. The sameness of a person or thing at all times and in all circumstances; the condition or fact that a person or thing is itself and not something else; individuality; personality.' Significantly, the OED separates 'personal identity' into a special category: 'the condition or fact of remaining the same person throughout the various phases of existence; continuity of the personality'. Despite the distinctions the dictionary imposes, however, it is clear that sameness and individuality or personality are intimately connected in all the definitions of identity. To have an identity, that is, to be unique, is to be the same in two senses: to be identical to others in your class and to be identical to yourself over time. The paradox at the root of identity is that sameness creates individuality and personality: being the same makes you different.

Philosophers, not surprisingly, have been intrigued by the problems of identity and the paradoxes embedded in it. Recent Anglo-American philosophy in particular has been concerned with what constitutes a human person and how we can identify that person as the same over time. Robert Nozick's recent work is a good example of the nature of this philosophical inquiry into identity. Nozick asserts: 'We want to understand not only the kind of being we are, but also what constitutes our individual identity as a particular being of that kind.' (Nozick, 1981, p.27.) His central concern is how we can identify a person over time. How, he asks, can we know that this person is the same as the person we knew yesterday, or last year? The answer he gives to this is what he calls the 'closest continuer': we can establish identity if we can ascertain that the person at t2 is the closest continuation of the person at t1 (Nozick, 1981, pp.36–7). Nozick's analysis of the closest continuer, although typical of the Anglo-American approach to identity, also reveals the underlying problem of that approach. Nozick spends a great deal of time trying to establish why it is that a person especially cares about his or her closest continuer without ever considering why this is such an odd question. Further problems emerge when Nozick turns to another issue: how do I know that the self-reflection that constitutes my identity is true rather than artificial? This question leads him to his now infamous tank case. He imagines a situation in which bodies are floating in a tank while psychologists stimulate their brains electronically to produce thoughts and experiences. How, Nozick then asks, can we be sure that this is not the case for us, that is, that our thoughts and experiences are not really our own? (Nozick, 1981, p.167.)

Many feminists have made the point that the concerns of philosophers such as Nozick are irrelevant to feminist questions of identity.[1] But the shortcomings of the contemporary Anglo-American philosophical approach to identity are not accidental. They are, rather, dictated by the paradoxes embedded in the concept of identity and its history in Western thought. Identity is necessarily about sameness and difference; it is about the intensely personal and the necessarily social.[2] But it is easy to lose sight of one side of the paradox while focusing on the other. The individual in theories such as Nozick's is disembodied and neutral. Neither sex nor gender enter into the construction of the individuals: they are not situated socially at all. This disembodied neutrality, however, is hardly unique. It has a long history in Western philosophy. Plato began the tradition by arguing that men and women are identical because souls are sexless.[3] In the modern era, in the guise of the abstract individual of the liberal tradition, this concept has become hegemonic; defining the individual as abstract, neutral, disembodied, and devoid of social context has become the hallmark of modernity. It is this definition that results in the bizarre analyses of philosophers such as Nozick. Asking why we should care about ourselves and whether we are really having our own experiences are questions that only make sense given this definition.

In the first wave of feminist critiques, theorists did not challenge the disembodied individual of the modernist tradition. First-wave theorists agreed with Plato that men and women are in essence identical; sexual differences were defined as superficial rather than constitutive. In the second wave of feminist critiques, however, the differences between men and women were emphasised and valorised; separate and distinct sexual identities were asserted. Despite significant differences between the first- and second-wave theories, however, two elements united them: an emphasis on social construction and a unified concept of sexual/gender identity. Both of these elements would prove to be problematic. Defining identity, especially sexual identity, as a product of social construction seems to be a complete repudiation of the disembodied, neutral individual. But, in application no such reversal occurred. It is a tribute to the hegemony of the modernist concept that focusing on social construction does not necessarily jettison the abstract individual. The presupposition of many feminist critiques of identity is a human body that is a blank slate on which social texts are written. Thus, social construction is posited on a neutral, abstract body that pre-exists the social. This conception replicates, rather than replaces, the abstract liberal individual; the locus of that abstract sameness is simply displaced. To deconstruct the disembodied concept of identity, feminists need a conception of human bodies as already relational and social, a relationality that precedes the social texts inscribed on these bodies.[4]

The concept of a unified sex/gender identity has also come under fire in recent feminist theorising. In the post-second-wave era, differences among women have come to the foreground. Even path-breaking second-wave theorists such as Carol Gilligan are exploring racial and class differences among women (Taylor, Gilligan and Sullivan, 1995). But all these explorations of differences, far from resolving the paradoxes of identity, have raised new questions. What, exactly, are we to make of all these different identities? What is to become of the identity of 'woman' that informed second-wave theories? Are our identities constructed or essential? Do we discover them or become determined by them?

That these questions have yet to be resolved and, consequently, that feminist accounts of identity are in a state of flux is indicated by a definition of identity offered by an introductory women's studies textbook: 'Our identity is a specific marker of how we define ourselves at any particular moment in life. Discovering and claiming our unique identity is a process of growth, change, renewal and regeneration throughout our lifetime. As a specific marker, identity may seem tangible and fixed at any given point. Over the life span, however, identity is more fluid.' (Kirk and Okagawa-Rey, 1997, p.51.) Although it may be inappropriate to demand philosophical clarity from an introductory textbook, this definition is indicative of a confusion over questions of identity that pervades contemporary feminist theory. The reference to 'discovering and claiming our unique identity' in the first sentence of the definition presupposes an essential identity that, although perhaps hidden, is there to be uncovered. But an essentialist definition of identity is then denied in the next two sentences. There the authors emphasise fluidity and change, rejecting a tangible, fixed identity. Putting these two understandings of identity together makes little sense, either epistemologically or experientially. We are enjoined to discover and claim our unique identity while at the same time understanding that this identity is fluid and intangible, that it will change over time. What is not addressed is how these two concepts of identity can be compatible.

The multiplicity of feminine identities has become a theme of third-wave feminist writing. Reading the accounts of third-wavers one is struck not only by the diversity of identities that are proclaimed, but also by the authors' silence on the question of the identity of 'woman' (Walker, 1995; Findlen, 1995). The celebration of diversity in these accounts, however, does little to resolve the difficult questions raised by this diversity. Indeed, they raise another set of problems: how do individuals cope with multiple identities that coexist in one individual? The author of one of these accounts, Sonja Curry-Johnson, confesses to an 'acute sense of multiplicity' (1995, p.222). The multiple identities that she feels define her also divide her. 'Each identity defines me; each is responsible for elements of my character; from each I devise some sustenance for my soul.' But these identities do not peacefully coexist. The effort to blend them together harmoniously she describes as 'desperate'. Curry-Johnson's article is, in some sense, a cry for help. She feels that women should be able to 'bring our full selves to the table'. But she also does not see how this could be made possible.

These third-wave accounts as well as the textbook definition of identity I referred to above reveal the contradictions at the root of contemporary feminist theories of identity. All of us need to experience our identity as *ours*, a continuity over time, something that places us in a particular time and place. But how can we incorporate this experiential aspect of identity with the other aspect of identity that emerges from contemporary feminist accounts, its fluidity and constructedness? How can we incorporate these seemingly contradictory elements into one concept, experiencing ourselves as both fixed and fluid? Furthermore, how can we reconcile the 'acute sense of multiplicity' that results from the array of different identities that present themselves to us? What differences make a difference?

One of the most comprehensive attempts to answer these questions, to deal with the inherent paradoxes of identity and difference is William Connolly's *Identity/Difference* (1991). Connolly's principal concern is to contest the tendency to establish identity by defining its opposite (other) as evil. He rightly defines this tendency as the source of regimes of political oppression, then goes on to counter this by defining a concept of identity that takes itself to be both historically contingent and inherently relational (Connolly, 1991, p.48). Central to his project is the concept is difference: 'Identity requires difference in order to be, and it conveys difference into otherness in order to secure its own self-certainty.' (Connolly, 1991, p.64.)

The connection between difference and otherness leads Connolly to an apparently contradictory conclusion: we can neither defend nor dispense with identities. On the one hand, he states, 'My identity is what I am and how I am recognized rather than what I choose, want or consent to. It is the dense self from which choosing, wanting and consenting proceed. Without that density, these acts could not occur; with it, they are recognized to be mine.' (Connolly, 1991, p.64.) This is the definition of identity that Connolly cannot dispense with. But it is also one that he cannot defend because, on his account, both personal and collective identities inevitably define themselves as true, converting differences into otherness and otherness into scapegoats (Connolly, 1991, p.67).

But although Connolly recognises both the necessity and the danger of identity, his solution is to place more weight on the danger than the necessity. Connolly's concept of identity comes down on the side of contingency. The kind of identity he advocates is ironic and ambiguous. It avoids the danger of otherness and scapegoating by embracing fluidity and construction/reconstruction. Politically, this entails a politics of 'contingent identity and ambiguous responsibility' (Connolly, 1991, p.121), a politics that problematises the tactics by which established identities protect themselves through the conversion of difference into otherness (Connolly, 1991, p.159).[5]

Connolly's resolution has informed many contemporary feminist accounts of identity. Cautions against the dangers of fixed identities abound in contemporary feminist theory. But there are serious liabilities to this resolution. In his attempt to counter the dangers of 'true identity' and the creation of otherness, Connolly overlooks the equally grave danger of ignoring the constitution of what he calls the 'dense self'. Connolly claims that he cannot dispense with identity, but he does precisely that in arguing exclusively for a politics of ambiguous identity. Against this I can use Connolly's own argument to assert that I need to know who I am before I can choose and act, politically or otherwise. Unless the process by which I do this is explained and incorporated into my definition of identity, I will have no identity to problematise.

Power, Politics and Identity

'Identity politics', although informed by contemporary theories of identity, raises a distinct set of issues around the topic of identity. I have argued that contemporary feminist theories of identity leave basic issues unanswered. The 'real world' of identity politics is, if anything, more confusing. On the face of it, it would seem that identity politics represents a significant advance for feminist politics. First-wave feminists accepted the neutral, disembodied citizen of the Western liberal tradition, arguing that women belonged in this category as well. One of the significant advances of second-wave feminism was to reveal the fallacy of this assumption. Feminists argued that the neutral, disembodied citizen was, in actuality, masculine, and, thus, that women could not assume the identity of 'citizen' in this polity.

Second-wave feminism's 'woman', however, did not provide the desired political solution for feminist politics. This 'woman' turned out to be white, heterosexual, middle-class, and aspiring to a professional career alongside her husband. The category of 'woman' did not encompass the diversity of women even within our society, much less non-Western women. It certainly did not encompass the women of colour who cleaned the professional woman's house and cared for her children.

From this perspective, identity politics seems to be the perfect solution for feminist politics. Identity politics offers a plethora of identities from which women can choose. Instead of being limited to one general and necessarily hierarchical category of 'woman', women can choose an identity that fits them, one that resonates with their particular situation. Identity politics has overcome the homogenising tendencies of second-wave feminism by acknowledging the differences among women and, most significantly, attacking the hierarchy concealed in the concept 'woman'.

But the problems for feminism implicit in identity politics are also becoming apparent. The first of these is that referred to by Connolly: the tendency to reify identity, to assume that it is true, fixed and given, rather than fluid and constructed. The fixing of identity appears to be an unavoidable by-product of identity politics. Entering the political arena by embracing a particular identity necessarily fixes that identity in both political and legal terms. Women who embrace the identity of a marginalised group are forced by the political process to accept that identity as their exclusive definition. Furthermore, if the goal of political activity is to seek legal redress for the group's marginalisation, the law will further serve to fix that identity. Identity politics is about granting *this* particular group of persons rights in the liberal polity. For this to be effective, the identity of the members of the group must be clear and definitive. Ambiguity and contingency do not translate into this political and legal milieu.

A second problem arises from the necessary connection between identity and difference. Differences always involve power; they are created and enforced by societies, governments, and institutions. As June Jordan so aptly puts it, 'There is difference and there is power. And who holds the power decides the meaning of the difference.' (Jordan, 1994, p.197.) The differences that identity politics embraces are the differences that society creates and enforces. Feminist identity politics represents a rebellion against the general category 'woman' that privileged white, middle-class women. Yet the identities that women have embraced under the rubric of identity politics are not of their own choosing, they are, rather, precisely those imposed by the society they are challenging. Feminism, as an oppositional politics, should be challenging rather than affirming the identities and differences of our polity. The effect of identity politics, however, is to reify rather than redefine those differences.[6]

There is no easy answer to this problem. The differences our language creates are, in a sense, all we have to go on. If we challenge those differences by asserting their opposites, the challenge is necessarily parasitic on the difference itself, not an escape from it. The goal of much of Judith Butler's work is to grapple with this problem. The difficulty of her formulations attests to the complexity of the problems that identity politics has created. Her most comprehensive attempt to summarise this problem is a typically opaque passage from *Bodies That Matter*:

> Doubtless crucial is the ability to wield signs of subordinated identity in a public domain that constitutes its own [for example] homophobic and racist hegemonies through the erasure or domestication of culturally and politically constituted identities. [But] ... insofar as it is imperative that we insist upon those specificities in order to expose the fictions of imperialist humanism that works through unmarked privilege [for example, the rationalist humanisms of Locke and Kant, Rawls and Habermas] there remains

> the risk that we will make the articulation of ever more specified identities the aim of political activism. [Rather than succumbing to this temptation] ... every insistence of identity must at some point lead to a taking stock of the constitutive exclusions that reconsolidate hegemonic power differentials, exclusions that each articulation was forced to make in order to proceed. This critical reflection will be important in order not to replicate at the level of identity politics the very exclusionary moves that initiated the turn to specific identities in the first place. (Butler, 1993, p.118.)

We are, in other words, damned if we do and damned if we do not. We must embrace excluded identities to contest hegemony, but in doing so we both reify that hegemony and fix the identities. Butler suggests a number of strategies to avoid both of these traps: multiple sites of contestation (1990, p.32); gender performances that both enact and reveal the perfomativity of gender (1990, p.139); and destabilising substantive identity (1990, p.146). That none of these strategies is simple or suggests an obvious political agenda is evidence of the difficulty of the problem. At the end of *Bodies That Matter* Butler asks: 'How will we know the difference between the power we promote and the power we oppose?' (Butler, 1993, p.241.). She seems to be acknowledging with this question that she has no clear answer to it.

Wendy Brown, in *States of Injury* (1995), also explores this problem and its implications for the politics of identity. While applauding identity politics as a deconstruction of collective identity, she argues that there are serious dangers involved in tying individuals to their legal definition. Identity politics rooted in these definitions fixes the identity of the political actors as injured, as victims. These identities originated in an effort to subordinate these subjects, not free them. From Brown's perspective, identity politics involves embracing and fixing the identity of the injured victim, an identity imposed and enforced by hegemonic political power. Such identities, she claims, cannot be liberative.[7]

A third problem is a corollary of a theoretical point frequently articulated by the critics of postmodern feminism. In their well-known article on feminism and postmodernism, Fraser and Nicholson (1990) castigated postmodernism for thwarting social critique. The multiplicity of sites fostered by postmodernism, they argued, obscures the larger picture of institutional control of social institutions. Other critics of the influence of postmodern feminism have argued that it promotes difference without differentiation. We need general social categories, these critics have argued, to engage in social critique of the hegemonic institutions of patriarchy (Bordo, 1990). This theoretical point also has practical political implications. There are concrete political benefits to be derived from general categories such as 'woman' and 'gender'. They allow feminists to focus their political energies on patriarchal institutions that harm all women. The demise of these categories and the emphasis on differences among women has diffused the opposition to masculinist organisations. The challenge of identity politics is how to use these categories to our benefit without losing the equally important benefit of acknowledging the differences among women.

Shane Phelan raises yet another problem in her discussion of identity politics from a lesbian perspective. She argues: 'What has been accepted in the lesbian community is not the lesbian but the *Lesbian* – the politically/sexually/culturally correct being, the carrier of *the* lesbian feminist consciousness.' (Phelan, 1989, p.57.) Phelan argues that this definition arose from the need to impose unity in the lesbian community. But, in the process of constructing this identity, any sense of the plurality of lesbian lives was lost. Phelan deplores this loss, arguing that we must focus on our differences as well as our commonalities. Without an understanding of the otherness of others, she asserts, we cannot do them justice as human agents. She concludes:

> Identity politics must be based, not on identity, but on the appreciation of politics as the art of living together. Politics that ignores our identities, that makes them 'private' is useless, but non-negotiable identities will enslave us whether they are imposed from within or without. (Phelan, 1989, p.170.)

Phelan's analysis reveals another dimension of Connolly's argument that fixing identities creates otherness and scapegoating. Phelan's point is that identities, even oppositional identities, can be just as restrictive as the collective identity imposed by the liberal polity, erasing multiplicity and individuality just as the liberal concept of 'citizen' does. Phelan wants to correct this without returning to what she defines as the privatisation of identity by liberalism. What Phelan's analysis overlooks, however, is a significant similarity between identity politics and liberal politics. The liberal polity does not privatise political identity, but, rather, imposes a singular identity on all citizens. Far from ignoring identity, liberalism demands conformity to the abstract liberal individual it defines as 'citizen'. Those who do not conform to this identity are excluded from politics by definition. In this sense, identity politics is not so much a departure from liberalism as a continuation of the identity politics liberalism inaugurated. The dispute is over *which* identities are politically appropriate not whether identity itself is politically appropriate.

The problem that Phelan identifies is even more graphically illustrated by the experience of pan-ethnic political movements in the USA. Ethnic groups are, in theory, voluntary collectives defined by national origin whose members share a distinctive, integrated culture. In practice, ethnic politics in the USA is something quite different. Political necessity has thrown together ethnic groups who, at best, have little in common and, at worst, have a history of ethnic hatred. Groups categorised as, for example, 'Asian' or 'Hispanic' are made up of diverse peoples; their designation is a result of the dominant group's inability or unwillingness to recognise their differences. The 'ethnic' movement that results is thus a product of the necessities of liberal politics and the legal categories created by that politics. It unites individuals with little or no 'natural' ethnic similarities and forces them to ignore their differences for political and legal purposes. Such a politics emphasises the constructed, political character of ethnic categories and the constitutive role of dominant institutions.[8]

The problems generated by identity politics in feminism have not gone unnoticed. Many solutions have been advanced that attempt to resolve these problems. One pole in this debate is that occupied by those who advocate acknowledging and embracing the fluidity and provisionality of identity without qualification. William Connolly's argument in *Identity/Difference* represents this pole. Shane Phelan applies this position directly to feminism in her sequel to *Identity Politics*, *Getting Specific* (1994). Lesbians, she argues, should enter politics as people occupying provisional subject positions. Phelan describes her position as an identity politics that rests on a de-essentialised concept of identity. She is not alone in advancing this position. Butler advocates an anti-foundational approach to identity politics that rejects a stable, unified, and agreed upon identity for women. Cornell West expresses the core of this position:

> Distinctive features of the new cultural politics of difference are: to trash the monolithic and homogeneous in the name of diversity, multiplicity and heterogeneity; to reject the abstract, general and universal in light of the concrete, specific and particular; and to historicize, contextualize and pluralize by highlighting the contingent, provisional, variable, tentative, shifting and changing. (West, 1995, p.147.)

The opposite pole in this debate is occupied by those who want to return to the collective identity of liberal theory, arguing that we need the protections it affords. The most forceful (and polemical) statement of this position is that of Jean Bethke Elshtain. Elshtain defines identity politics as the replacement of public ends and purposes with private identity: 'The citizen gives way before the aggrieved member of a self-defined or contained group.' (Elshtain, 1995, p.53.) The problem with identity politics, she argues, is that rather than negotiating the complexity of public and private identities, the participants in identity politics disdain any distinction between the citizen and whatever else they may be, for example, female, gay, disabled, and so on. But these differences, Elshtain asserts, are not civically interesting. In a rhetorical flourish, she identifies the efforts to 'retribalise' into ethnic or other groups as the cause of the disappearance of democracy, 'as so much froth on the polluted sea of phony equality' (Elshtain, 1995, p.74).

In the course of arguing for one pole in this dispute, however, Elshtain reveals a curious phenomenon that has emerged in the debate: the convergence of the two poles on key issues. Elshtain points out that the adherents of the politics of difference advance their own version of sameness: the 'different' identities they assert are singular, not multiple (1995, p.75). Phelan argued this point in her earlier book, identifying this tendency as a weakness in the politics of identity; Connolly does the same. But although the theorists of identity politics reject fixed identities, it is nevertheless the case that in practice this almost inevitably occurs. Thus, in the political arena, the two poles of the argument converge precisely on the question of identity. Both the critics and the advocates of identity politics claim that a particular kind of identity is a prerequisite for political action; for both, politics is intimately connected to identity. In addition, the advocates of both sides presuppose a particular structure of the political arena that political identities inhabit. Sheldon Wolin makes this point in his analysis of the politics of difference. This politics, he asserts, necessarily appeals to the presuppositions of collectivity to accomplish its purposes. Like the liberal polity that it opposes, it must presuppose a democratic practice capable of respecting differences and responding to grievances (Wolin, 1993, p.480).

One of the ironies of identity politics is that the malleability of identity is both revealed and denied by the practice of identity politics. Those who actually engage in identity politics are forced by political and legal necessity to fix identity in precisely the way that the theorists deplore. But their very presence in the political arena attests to the malleability of identities. The 'injured' identities that they embrace are, as Brown argues, constructs of the hegemonic political powers they oppose. Participants in identity politics attempt to reconstruct these identities in a positive direction. Thus, 'Black power' replaces the black as second-class citizen and 'differently abled' replaces 'handicapped' or 'disabled'. In the course of political engagement, however, these new constructions of identity become just as fixed as the identity constructs they replace.

The conflict between the two poles in the debate over identity politics has, not surprisingly, also generated attempts to stake out a middle ground on these issues. A number of themes have emerged from these attempts. The first is defining a pragmatic post-identity politics, a sort of identity politics without the identity. Thus, Wendy Brown advocates replacing the politics of difference with the politics of diversity (1995, p.51). What she means by this is that differences are grasped from a perspective larger than one position, more inclusive than that offered by a single identity. Brown advocates a politics of 'I want this for us', rather than a politics of 'I am'.[9]

Iris Young also advocates a feminist politics that emphasises pragmatic goals rather than identity. Young borrows Sartre's concept of seriality to argue that we can claim identity, even an identity as broad as the collectives 'woman' or 'gender', not as a set of essential attributes, but as a social collective whose members are unified passively by the relations their actions have to material objects (1997). The emphasis here is on practical politics, attaining concrete objectives, rather than expressing essential or ontological meanings.[10]

A second theme of post-identity politics is the claim that politics must necessarily be redefined in its wake. Thus, Susan Bickford (1996) argues that neither liberals nor communitarians can do justice to the complexity of identity. We are not the identical citizens of liberalism, but, because we belong to multiple, overlapping communities, communitarian descriptions fail as well.[11] But Bickford does not see the postmodern theory of identity as a viable alternative. She argues that the postmodern definition of identity as a fiction (constantly under construction, fluid, provisional, and contingent) is a political liability rather than a solution. We need identity, she argues, because political purposes are articulated by beings who understand themselves as human subjects with various social identities. Identities carry with them constraint and oppression, but also a source of criticism and action. Without denying that identities are created, Bickford wants to characterise this creation as active rather than passive, a matter of agency rather than subjection (1996, pp.116–24). Along with the other post-identity theorists, Bickford argues that what feminism needs is a new politics that can deal with the complexities of identity. The question of what that politics might be, however, remains unanswered.

Negotiating Identity

I began this discussion of the question of identity in contemporary feminist theory with Linda Alcoff's 1988 article not because she has a particularly insightful perspective on identity, but because it provides an important context for contemporary discussions of identity. Alcoff defines the crucial issue facing feminist theory in the late twentieth century: defining a new paradigm for feminism that eschews modernist dichotomies and articulates a new conception of knowledge and the self. Alcoff's subsequent work is a testimony to the importance of this objective. Her *Real Knowing* (1996) is a significant step toward the definition of that paradigm.

The current 'identity crisis' has sidetracked this effort to define a new paradigm. The theorists of identity politics advocate a conception of identity as fluid and fictitious, but this conception does not resonate with political actors. Those engaged in identity politics, on the other hand, have turned toward an essentialism that is the antithesis of the theorists' conception. The options available to feminist theory and politics in the wake of identity politics, furthermore, are all flawed in important ways. The first option, that embraced by first-wave feminism and advocated by theorists such as Elshtain, is to adopt the neutral, disembodied identity of Western liberalism, and, by extension, modernism itself. Several decades of feminist scholarship have revealed that this disembodied, neutral individual is inherently rather than accidentally masculine. Returning to this conception solves the question of the relationship between identity and politics by excluding women from citizenship. Women, in this conception, simply do not have the equipment to be citizens, moral agents, or even full human beings.

The second option, that embraced by second-wave feminism, is to define and valorise the general category 'woman'. One of the distinct advantages of the current emphasis on differences among women is to reveal the liabilities of this conception. 'Woman' privileges a certain group of women, just as 'citizen' privileges a certain category of men. Although feminists are beginning to realise that there are advantages to the utilisation of general categories in both theory and practice, returning to the identity 'woman' has too many liabilities to make it a viable option.

The reaction against the second-wave conception of 'woman', the advent of identity politics, and the increasing influence of postmodernism and post-structuralism have created two additional options. The first is the theoretical position on identity arising from the postmodern/post-structuralist critique of identity as a modernist fiction. Identity here is contingent, fluid, constructed; any hint of essentialism is rejected. The second 'post-woman' option is that embraced by women in the political arena. The identities that these women proclaim are identities that predate identity politics, but, their adherents claim, have been transformed from negatives into positives, providing sites for political action and change.

That both of these options are also flawed has become increasingly obvious in recent years. On an epistemological level, the arguments for constructed identity are irrefutable. Even those who argue for a general category of 'woman' in contemporary feminism do not define identity as the discovery of an essential core. That identities are constructed from the mix of elements available in a given society is the only explanation for vast cultural variations in identity. But theories of constructed identity, despite this underlying strength, are inadequate in several important respects. There are significant theoretical gaps in this approach that its advocates, both feminist and non-feminist, have not addressed.

Chief among these is attention to what I will call the experiential dimension of identity and an understanding of the necessary distinction between the epistemological analysis of identity and the experience of identity in everyday life. Although I may know, on an epistemological level, that my identity is constructed from the mix of elements in my particular society, I do not, and, I think, cannot, experience my identity as this fluid construction. On the level of experience, I must know myself as a stable self, as the entity that provides continuity to the disparate elements of my life, as the deep self who makes choice possible. One way of putting this is that my philosophical/epistemological knowledge of my identity is one language game, my everyday experience of myself is another. Both are important, but mixing the language games creates a dangerous confusion. Attention to this experiential element is almost entirely missing from the accounts of identity offered by postmoderns and post-structuralists that have been so influential in feminist theory.

This failure is responsible for much of the reaction against the theory of constructed identity in the feminist community. The widespread objections to Judith Butler's theory of gender as performance are emblematic of that reaction. Many feminists found this definition of gender offensive, as a violation of their understanding of the experience of gender in their lives. Surely, Butler's critics argued, gender must be more central to my identity than the clothes I wear, than my performance in a particular role. Butler's theory of identity provides the clearest example of the liability of the postmodern/post-structuralist approach. She brilliantly deconstructs the notion of the coherent, stable self and then concludes that the exact opposite must be the case: there is no being behind the doing. What she fails to consider is the possibility of a middle ground between these two extremes: a sense of identity that, although constructed, is a stable and necessary component of human selfhood and agency. Although, in an epistemological sense, identity may be, as she puts it, a 'necessary error' (Butler, 1993, p.229), in everyday life, it is simply a necessity.

Another aspect of the experiential difficulty of embracing a contingent identity is evident in Richard Rorty's work. In *Contingency, Irony, and Solidarity*, Rorty argues that embracing a non-essentialist position need not cause any problems for the coherency of individual actions. Specifically, he argues that beliefs can regulate action and even be worth dying for, even if those who hold them are aware that they are caused by nothing deeper than contingent circumstances (Rorty, 1989, p.189). Individuals do not, in fact, die for principles they regard as contingent, much less constructed, fluid, or fictional. On the contrary, they die for beliefs that they know to be linked to their deep selves, that are connected to who they know themselves to be. Contingency will not bring me to the barricades.

Perhaps the most devastating critique of the constructed self, particularly as it is expressed in postmodern literature, is that of James Glass. In *Shattered Selves* (1993), Glass argues that the postmodern conception of self and identity is, quite literally, dangerous: it describes the fragmented, shattered selves of multiple-personality disorders. His argument is directed specifically against the postmodern theorists who advocate a playful, creative approach to identity, and, most importantly, define schizophrenia and multiple personalities as liberative deconstructions of identity. Against this, Glass argues that fragmented, shattered identities are evidence of pain, not liberation. Commenting on one victim of multiple personalities, he asserts: 'Hers is not a liberatory, playful experience; her multiple realities annihilate the self's emotional possibility, destroy the psychological foundations of consent, shatter the shared experiences of historical knowledge.' (Glass, 1993, p.46.)

Glass's conclusions are drawn from research he conducted on women suffering from schizophrenia and multiple-personality disorder. The pain that these women suffer is palpable; the disorientation of their lives is difficult to read about, much less experience. Glass makes a strong case that the unity of the self is both a difficult achievement and a necessary requirement for leading any version of a good and satisfying life. A stable identity, he argues, is necessary because it 'locates the self in the world; it defines emotional and interpersonal knowledge; it frames the self in a historical and situational context' (Glass, 1993, p.48). Glass concludes that utilising schizophrenia or other identity disorders as an ideal deconstructed identity is irresponsible and insensitive to the human costs of these illnesses.

There is much that is wrong with Glass's critique. Theorists such as Deleuze and Guattari define schizophrenia as a social institution that is both a product of capitalism and the possibility of its overthrow (1977). They do not, as Glass concludes, advocate that, in a literal sense, we become schizophrenics as that term is understood in psychology. Despite this, however, Glass's point is valid on another level. His thesis is that I must necessarily experience myself as a coherent entity, historically located and contingent, but enduring through time. This self allows me to place myself in my historical context, to cope with the contingency of my existence. To experience this self not as the frame of my contingent existence, but itself radically contingent is, as Glass argues, to court madness.

The second 'post-woman' option in feminist politics swings the pendulum in the opposite direction. The desire to transform the inferior identities that have excluded groups from the political arena is at the root of contemporary identity politics. This is the source of Wendy Brown's categorisation of identity politics as a politics of injury. The political participation of those engaged in identity politics is predicated on the affirmation of a new identity that, although related to that injury, transforms it. It is on the basis of this identity that they demand equality and recognition in the political arena.

The problem with this option is that, as its many critics have argued, proclaiming an identity, even a marginalised identity, almost inevitably leads to the fixing of that identity. Identity politics is a politics that graphically illustrates how identities change and are reconstructed under different social conditions and yet it almost invariably leads, in practice, to a repudiation of construction. The identities of identity politics, despite their multiplicity in the political arena, can be just as oppressive as those they replace. 'The Lesbian', 'the Asian' or 'the Hispanic' is a creation of political necessity, a construction that erases differences within the category. Identity is not tailored to individual identities, nor does it recognise identities as fluid and constructed. On the contrary, it fixes identity in a new location.

If all the available options for the construction of identity are flawed, then what direction should feminist politics take? Is there an identity politics that is viable for feminism? I think the answer to the first question is that social constructionist theories of identity can be adapted to feminist needs. The social construction of identity must be a central element of the new paradigm that feminism is constructing. But the parameters of that social construction must be carefully delineated; feminists must adopt theories of identity to their specifically feminist concerns. The first element of that feminist redefinition is an emphasis on agency. As Foucault and many others have argued, social construction does not entail social dupes. Agency is not a product of our universal, essential humanity. It is, rather, a product of socially constructed identity, a resource that is produced in varying discursive formations. Socially constructed selves are not social dupes, but agents who act and resist. This aspect of the social construction of identity is often overlooked by its critics. But it is both compatible with social construction and a necessary element of any feminist, and, hence, oppositional, approach to identity and social construction.

The second element of the feminist redefinition of identity relates to Foucault's claim that identity is a work of art (1983, p.237). Foucault argued that we construct our identities from the mix of possibilities available to us in our social/discursive situation. But defining the self as a work of art leaves out several crucial considerations that are central to feminist concerns. What if the available identity options are so limited that they provide no possibility of constructing a satisfying identity? What if my only options are to be an obedient or a disobedient slave? Foucault's formulation sounds almost offensive in this context. It is only the privileged who can choose an aesthetic mix of identity options in constructing a self. To describe the identity constructions of the disprivileged as a work of art is not only misleading, but condescending. This aspect of Foucault's work reveals his blindness toward the functioning of certain aspects of power. In his zeal to find power everywhere, he ignores the fact that subjects are affected by power in differential ways.

Closely related to this is the third element necessary for a feminist redefinition of the social constructionist theory: an analysis of the role of hegemonic identities. Gender, race, and class are, in a sense, hyper-identities, identities that individuals cannot choose to reject wholesale. Another way of putting this is that no matter which identity I choose, these hyper-identities will always be a part of my identity. If I choose to be a medical doctor, I will be a *woman* doctor, not just a doctor. Feminist analyses of identity must not lose sight of the fact that all aspects of identity are not equal: some are frivolous and inconsequential, while others are all-pervasive and life-altering. As many of the feminist theorists discussed above have emphasised, there are those who have power and those who do not. Those who do not are not free to choose what differences are going to matter; certain differences matter because those in power enforce them. One way of interpreting the mentally disturbed women that Glass investigated is that the identity options available to them as women were all unsatisfactory and, as a result, their identity itself fragmented.

The fourth aspect of identity that must be incorporated into the feminist concept is the experiential dimension discussed above. As Glass and even Connolly argue, we must have a coherent self who does the choosing that constitutes an identity. This coherent self is missing in many postmodern and feminist accounts of identity that emphasise social construction. Social constructionist theorists of identity provide a satisfying explanation from an epistemological perspective. Identities are constructed from the social/discursive mix available to me in my contingent historical circumstances. Likewise, many identity options are closed to me because of those circumstances; my range of options may be large or radically circumscribed depending on those circumstances.

But my everyday experience of my identity is not the same as my epistemological understanding of it. Confusing these different language games can lead to serious confusions about identity. As a feminist political theorist, I know, in an epistemological sense, that incorporating the identity 'feminist' was a possibility for me because of my class, race, education, age, and location in the USA in the 1960s and 1970s. I embraced an identity that became a possibility for particularly located women in this time and place: feminist. This identity was not available to some women; it was not as widely available in earlier periods. I was at the right place at the right time to become a feminist.

My experience of acquiring this identity, however, was quite different. I did not experience 'feminist' as an identity that I decided to adopt simply because it was contingently available to me. Rather, I encountered feminism as a discovery of who I really am, as a revelation, something that resonated with my experience of myself. I did not experience myself as choosing to adopt feminism rather than some other identity I might have chosen, but, rather, as a logical extension of a pre-existing 'I'.

It is this overlooked dimension of identity that has, more than anything, compromised postmodern and post-structuralist feminist accounts of identity. These accounts are irrefutable on the epistemological level. But identity is not just about epistemology, it is also about experience. Both language games are necessary to an understanding of identity. Without attending to the experiential dimension of identity we cannot formulate a conception of selves functioning in the world. Although both Connolly (the dense self) and Butler (the necessary error of identity) recognise this aspect of identity, they ultimately reject it because they fear the dangers it incurs. I am arguing that it is just as dangerous to reject this aspect of identity, that without it our understanding is incomplete.

With these feminist corrections to social constructionist theories of identity, then, this approach can serve feminism well. The question of whether there is an identity politics that is viable for feminism, however, is another matter. The best option for feminist politics in the wake of identity politics is not so much the 'post-identity' politics that Brown and others have advocated, but a politics that eschews identity altogether. Identity politics has derailed feminist thought and mired it in a maze of contradictions. Identity politics is not a solution for feminism and, similarly, there is no solution to the problems it poses because it harks back to the politics of modernism/liberalism. For liberalism, identity is central to politics, it is a requirement for political participation. Although identity politics radically redefines political identity, it continues this tradition by making identity central to politics. It thus perpetuates, rather than transcends, that politics.

My advocacy of a feminist politics beyond identity contains two elements. First, it entails contesting a politics that requires a singular identity for full citizenship. Second-wave feminism was right in this case. The neutral, disembodied citizen of liberalism (who was, of course, neither) excluded women and others who did not fit the definition. We must eschew this identity and any attempt to impose an identity that excludes certain categories of individuals from political participation. The second element of my argument is that political participation should not be predicated on *any* conception of identity, even if a diverse array of identities is available. The old politics of liberalism/modernism was about identity, the new politics of feminism should not be. As the experience of identity politics has shown, there is no viable way to define identity in political terms – doing so inevitably entails fixing identities. Defining identities is a slippery slope; any definition will erase differences within the category that is constructed; ultimately, each of us has a unique identity. The political conclusion for feminism must be a non-identity politics that defines politics in terms of pragmatic political action and accomplishing concrete political goals.

My position does not entail, however, what critics have called the privatisation of identity. It is misleading to claim that the liberal polity privatised identity. Liberalism imposed an identity on individuals that either allowed or disallowed equal political participation. It privatised differences within the identity of universal citizen, not identity itself. Identity politics replicates this in that it demands a particular identity for political participation and imposes identities that erase differences by fixing identity. Significantly, theorists from both sides of the identity debate argue that such an imposition is oppressive. The post-identity politics that I am advocating is one that neither imposes a singular identity nor requires particular identities for political actors. Saying 'no' to identity in both these cases is, I think, the best answer to identity politics.

NOTES

1. See Brison (1997) for a critique of Anglo-American philosophers' approach to identity.
2. See Ricoeur (1992).
3. See Allen (1997) for an analysis of Western approaches to the concept of woman.
4. See Moira Gatens (1996) for an insightful analysis of this issue. Also see Grosz (1994).
5. See also Oliver (1997).
6. See Scott (1995) for an analysis of these questions.
7. See Hirschmann (1996) and Lurie (1997).
8. For an insightful discussion of the pan-Asian political movement, see Espiritu (1992).
9. Martha Minow embraces Brown's position in Not Only for Myself (1997).
10. Felski makes a similar argument (1997).
11. See also Phillips (1994) and Aronowitz (1995).

REFERENCES

Alcoff, L. 1988. Cultural feminism versus post-structuralism: the identity crisis in feminist theory. *Signs*, 13 (3), pp.405–36.

1996. *Real Knowing*. Ithaca, Cornell University Press.

Allen, Sister Prudence. 1997. *The Concept of Woman: the Aristotelian Revolution 750BC–AD 1250*. Grand Rapids, Eerdman's.

Aronowitz, S. 1995. Reflections on identity. In *The Identity in Question*, ed. J. Rajchman, pp.111–27. New York, Routledge.

Bickford, S. 1996. *The Dissonance of Democracy: Listening, Conflict and Citizenship*. Ithaca, Cornell University Press.

Bordo, S. 1990. Feminism, postmodernism, and gender-scepticism. In *Feminism/Postmodernism*, ed. L. Nicholson, pp.133–76. New York, Routledge.

Brison, S. 1997. Outliving oneself: trauma, memory, and personal identity. In *Feminists Theorize the Political*, ed. D. Meyers, pp.12–39. Boulder, Westview.

Brown, W. 1995. *States of Injury: Power and Freedom in Late Modernity*. Princeton, Princeton University Press.

Butler, J. 1990. *Gender Trouble: Feminism and the Subversion of Identity*. New York, Routledge.

1993. *Bodies That Matter*. New York, Routledge.

Connolly, W. 1991. *Identity/Difference: Democratic Negotiations of Political Paradox*. Ithaca, Cornell University Press.

Curry-Johnson, S. 1995. Weaving an identity tapestry. In *Listen Up: Voices from the Next Feminist Generation*, ed. B. Findlen, pp.221–29. Seattle, Seal Press.

Deleuze, G. and Guattari F. 1977. *Anti-Oedipus: Capitalism and Schizophrenia*. New York, Viking Press.

Elshtain, J. B. 1995. *Democracy on Trial*. New York, Basic Books.

Espiritu, Yen Le. 1992. *Asian American Panethnicity: Bridging Institutions and Identities*. Philadelphia, Temple University Press.

Felski, R. 1997. The doxa of difference. *Signs*, 23 (1), pp.1–21.

Findlen, B. ed. 1995. Listen Up: Voices from the Next Feminist Generation. Seattle, Seal Press.

Foucault, M. 1983. On the genealogy of ethics: an overview of work in progress. In *Michel Foucault: Beyond Structuralism and Hermeneutics*, ed. H. Dreyfuss and P. Rabinow, second edn., pp.229–52. Chicago, University of Chicago Press.

Fraser, N. and Nicholson, L. 1990. Social criticism without philosophy: an encounter between feminism and postmodernism. In *Feminism/Postmodernism*, ed. L. Nicholson, pp.19–38. New York, Routledge.

Gatens, M. 1996. *Imaginary Bodies: Ethics, Power and Corporeality*. New York, Routledge.

Glass, J. M. 1993. *Shattered Selves: Multiple Personality in a Postmodern World*. Ithaca, Cornell University Press.

Grosz, E. 1994. *Volatile Bodies: Toward a Corporeal Feminism*. Bloomington, Indiana University Press.

Hirschmann, N. 1996. Revisioning freedom: relationship, context, and the politics of empowerment. In *Revisioning the Political*, eds. N. Hirschmann and C. Di Stefano, pp.51–74. Boulder, Westview.

Jordon, J. 1994. *Technical Difficulties*. Boston, Beacon Press.

Kirk, G. and Okazawa-Rey, M. 1997. *Women's Lives: Multicultural Perspectives*. Mountain View (CA), Mayfield Publishing Co.

Lurie, S. 1997. *Unsettled Subjects: Restoring Feminist Politics to Poststructuralist Critique*. Durham, Duke University Press.

Minow, M. 1997. *Not Only for Myself: Identity, Politics and the Law*. New York, New Press.

Nozick, R. 1981. *Philosophical Explanations*. Cambridge, Harvard University Press.

Nussbaum, M. 1992. Human functioning and social justice: in defense of Aristotelian essentialism. *Political Theory*, 20 (2), pp.202–46.

Okin, S. M. 1994. Gender inequality and cultural differences. *Political Theory*, 22 (1), pp.5–24.

Oliver, K. 1997. *Family Values: Subjects Between Nature and Culture*. New York, Routledge.

Phelan, S. 1989. *Identity Politics*. Philadelphia, Temple University Press.

1994. *Getting Specific: Postmodern Lesbian Politics*. Minneapolis, University of Minnesota Press.

Phillips, A. 1994. *The Politics of Presence*. Oxford, Clarendon Press.

Ricoeur, P. 1992. *Oneself as Another*. Chicago, University of Chicago Press.

Rorty, R. 1989. *Contingency, Irony, and Solidarity*. New York, Cambridge University Press.

Scott, J. 1995. Multiculturalism and the politics of identity. In *The Identity in Question*, ed. J. Rajchman, pp.3–12, 21–31. New York, Routledge.

Taylor, J., Gilligan, C. and Sullivan, A. 1995. *Between Voice and Silence: Women and Girls, Race and Relationship*. Cambridge, Harvard University Press.

Walker, R., ed. 1995. *To Be Real: Telling the Truth and Changing the Face of Feminism*. New York, Doubleday.

West, C. 1995. The new cultural politics of difference. In *The Identity in Question*, ed. J. Rajchman, pp.147–71. New York, Routledge.

Wolin, S. 1993. Democracy, difference and re-cognition. *Political Theory*, 21 (3), pp.464–83.

Young, I. M. 1994. Gender as seriality: thinking about women as a social collective. *Signs*, 19 (3), pp.713–38.

1997. *Intersecting Voices: Dilemmas of Gender, Political Philosophy*, and Policy. Princeton, Princeton University Press.

2

Difference as an Occasion for Rights: A Feminist Rethinking of Rights, Liberalism, and Difference

NANCY J. HIRSCHMANN

In the debates within feminism over identity and difference, among all the diverse forms that feminism takes, the 'equality versus difference debate' has long occupied (and some would say stalled) feminist political and intellectual energy on a host of issues ranging from employment-related matters such as pregnancy leave and sexual harassment to pornography, to welfare. On the one hand are those who acknowledge that substantive differences among women in terms of race, class, sexuality, age, ethnicity, and nationality mean that 'feminism', if it is to be true to its claim to be representative of and dedicated to the welfare of all women, must reflect this diversity. On the other are those who believe that such attention to diversity, while admirable, is politically self-defeating, because the power necessary for political change requires at least a relatively united front.

This debate has related importantly to the historical and political connections between feminism and liberalism, for the emphasis on difference and its relation to equality has been central to the dilemma of women's treatment by and within the patriarchal liberal state. Historically, it has been the focal point for the denial of central liberal ideals of equality and freedom to women, from Locke's (1964) reluctant admissions about 'women's lot' to resistance to women's suffrage, to contemporary Supreme Court cases. Yet the principles of liberalism are supposedly consonant with difference; the whole idea of equal freedom is that we all have our own 'passions and interests', our own life projects, and we differ in our views, beliefs, and opinions. The liberal state is seen as the protector of such difference through the guarantee of rights. Indeed, it is often argued that liberalism gave feminism its founding political projects. It was the Enlightenment ideals of equality and freedom that provided early feminists such as

Mary Astell (1970), Mary Wollstonecraft (1985), and Harriet Taylor (1970) with the opening they needed to assert women's entitlement to be recognised as human subjects with agency and intellect despite their 'differences' from men. In creating the idea of individual agency for men, liberalism offered women a way to challenge patriarchy's denial of agency to women, a challenge that carries into contemporary feminism as well.

Yet, since it ushered in the 'second wave' of feminism in the early 1970s, liberalism has also been highly criticised by many feminists, who have maintained that its emphasis on individualism belies women's historical embeddedness in relationship, that its focus on freedom ignores women's activities of care in the family, and that its individualism and rights were constructed specifically for propertied white men and are sustainable only through the subservience of white women, landless workers, and people of colour (Jaggar, 1983; Pateman, 1988). Feminists and other critics point out that, despite liberalism's overt attention to diversity, liberal principles have historically been used to erase difference, in that only some interests, views, and life plans are seen as worthy by the state and hence protected by rights. In the early social contract theories, for instance, the theoretical centrality of choice is repeatedly undermined by theories of rationality and virtue that legitimate only certain choices and not others. If agents do not make the 'correct' choices (which always happen to be defined in coherence with the interests of economically privileged white men), irrationality is presumed and safety mechanisms, ranging from Hobbes's (1968) 'rational fiat' (Hirschmann, 1992, p.36) to Locke's 'tacit consent' to Rousseau's '*forcer d'etre libre*' to Rawls's (1971) 'original position' and 'veil of ignorance', are triggered to guarantee that everyone will 'consent' to whatever government, principles, and laws that the political theorist advocates (Pateman, 1979).

For women, difference has seemed even more irreconcilable with liberalism, for gender difference in particular is cast as the opposite of equality, such that women's bodily specificity must either be ignored in order to claim equal rights (as was the case in *California Federal Savings and Loan* v. *Guerra*) or else acknowledged, but denied equal rights (as happened in *The EEOC* v. *Sears*) (Eisenstein, 1989). The extreme difficulty that women have had in obtaining equality in liberal terms in the workplace, public policy, and the courts has justified many feminists in their rejection of liberalism as an inherently classist, racist, and sexist ideology. Indeed, many blame liberalism for feminism's own difficulties, particularly its tendency to talk in quasi-universal terms of 'women', which allows middle-class heterosexual white women to deny that they are really only talking about themselves and are excluding the experiences and needs of women of colour, lesbians, and poor women (hooks, 1984). As various branches within feminism have increasingly emphasised the notion of difference (both differences among women and women's differences from men), efforts to reconcile feminism with liberalism have come to be seen as inevitably proscribed by, and theoretically indebted to, its racist and classist origins. Notions of abstract universalism that lie at the heart of (patriarchal) liberal rights presuppose, and indeed require, sameness.

That assumption of sameness has been at the root of women's historical difficulty in accessing and using rights – the truly innovative and arguably most important, if not standard-bearing, contribution of liberalism to the modern political world – to their advantage. The connection between 'liberalism' and 'rights' is correctly seen as inseparable (Flathman, 1976, p.34). But this connection has led many anti-liberal feminists to reject rights as fundamentally patriarchal and inappropriate to feminist politics and theory that is interested in equality both among women and with men and that can accommodate the vast diversity among women (not to mention among men). If the reconciliation of equality and difference is to be attempted, liberalism in general, and rights in particular, would seem to have to be chucked.

However, in this essay, I want to argue against a flat-out rejection of the category of rights, and in favour of a feminist reformulation of rights that addresses and accommodates feminist concerns of difference, particularity, context, and identity. Part of this reformulation will involve a reconsideration of liberalism from a feminist perspective, but my major goal will be to see if the central liberal category of rights can be recuperated to explicitly feminist ends without being caught up in the often paradoxical and self-defeating problems in which liberal feminist rights advocacy is often mired. Focusing on difference from a feminist perspective can help us understand the historical necessity of women's exclusion from rights and how this exclusion makes the application of liberal rights to women problematic; but I hope it will also point the way to a reconfiguration of rights, as well as of central rights categories such as freedom, equality, the individual, neutrality, and universality, that allows for a fuller and more complex realisation of difference within a rights framework. By advocating an approach to rights that demands attention to particularity and specificity of need, feminism can present a stronger respect for difference but not give up the power that rights can often afford the politically disadvantaged.

Moreover, I want to take the somewhat paradoxical move of developing this vision through the work of Carol Gilligan, whose 'care model' of ethics has importantly motivated much feminist rejection of rights. I admit that given the individualistic history of 'rights' in the West, viewing care as a basis for rights seems rather counter-intuitive and impracticable. Indeed, Gilligan is generally seen as the Antichrist of rights talk, because care is seen as rejecting everything rights embody, such as universality, neutrality, and impartiality. But I believe there is a rights potential in the care response, a potential that enables feminists to reconstruct the concept of rights in a way that incorporates many important elements that feminists of a variety of stripes have retained from liberalism, while simultaneously addressing issues of difference and identity that are seen as entailing liberalism's rejection. Difference should not be seen as providing an excuse to deny rights to particular individuals or groups, as has often been the case for women under (patriarchal) liberalism, which insists that women must either base their claims to equal rights on assertions of sameness with men or assert their differences by abandoning claims to rights. Rather, difference should be seen as an *occasion for* rights, as a signal light indicating times when rights are particularly at issue; it marks out occasions when misunderstanding and conflict may arise and indicates the possibility for appropriate state protection that rights afford.

Feminism, Liberalism, and Rights: an Ambivalent Alliance

The standard liberal view of rights is to consider them as claims on others. Stemming back at least to the state-of-nature social contract theorists, most famously Hobbes and Locke, rights were conceived as civil (and for some, such as Locke, also natural) grantings of power that applied to individuals exclusively (Flathman, 1976, pp.1–2, 165 *passim*). Individuals were conceived as separate and distinct from all others, with relationships possible only by chosen agreement (or in Hobbes's case, sometimes by force, which in his view amounted to the same thing). Moreover, these 'individuals' were for the most part propertied white men. Over the centuries, 'groups' have had success in utilising rights claims, such as the class-action suits against Dupont by women whose health was adversely affected by silicone breast implants, or when environmental groups sue companies for pollution, or when a neo-Nazi group asserts the right to march in a town with a substantial

Jewish population. Despite the fact that rights can be accessed and used by groups and corporations, however, the notion of a right as an antagonistic claim is fundamentally individualist. Within the classical liberal view of rights, a right is a claim, a 'warrant' (Flathman, 1976, pp.62, 161),[1] and even a 'trump' (Dworkin, 1977). It is thus conceived as a kind of weapon, something that individuals (or more commonly, their attorneys) can use to beat back the claims of competing individuals. It is the Hobbesian state of war put into the context of civil society.[2]

Decades of feminist critique of liberal theory have compelled most feminists, and many non-feminists as well, to recognise the racist, classist, and sexist history of rights: its initial institutional application only to propertied white men; its definition of key concepts such as property and equality in ways that not only left out white women and people of colour, but depended on their subservience and classified them as forms of property; and its conceptualisation of individualism that ignored the importance of the relationship and connectedness that women's lives ensured. The guiding assumptions, political values, linguistic meanings, and discursive formations of the traditional liberal vision of rights all are premised and built upon a history of exclusion of white women, men and women of colour, and the poor.[3] This theoretical bias that academic feminists have identified coheres with a practical bias, for the extreme difficulty that white women, men and women of colour, and the poor have had in obtaining equality in liberal terms in the workplace, the courts, and public policy, including welfare policy and health insurance, has justified many feminists in their rejection of rights as an inherently classist, racist, and sexist ideology that has the subjection of poor women, and perhaps in particular poor Black women, at its core.

Of course, 'rights' do not constitute the whole of 'liberalism', but this rejection of rights has been closely tied to a much broader and extremely powerful rejection of liberalism by feminists from a wide range of political and theoretical frameworks. Despite this, however, feminists keep getting drawn back to liberalism in some form. Most feminists at least implicitly agree that the *ideals* of freedom and equality, so central to historical liberalism, are also historically important to women, who have been systematically denied equality under the law and the freedom to control their lives, make choices, and act as agents in the world. Certainly, the question of how one defines these concepts is crucial to both feminism and liberalism;[4] even the most severe totalitarianism can claim to preserve a particular conception of freedom and equality, as Isaiah Berlin (1971) has argued. But it also suggests that, at the very least, certain *aspects* of liberalism – the importance of individuality and difference, the notion that individuals have social and political meaning and significance, and the need for people to exert at least some degree of control over their bodies, relationships, and lives – are vital to most, if not all, kinds of feminism.

Indeed, in recent years, some feminists and others on the left have sought to reconcile liberalism with feminism and its often allied ideology of socialism. Notions of 'group rights', of 'communal individuality' and 'self-in-relationship' are used to reconcile feminist (and other) suspicions of the sexist and racist heritage of liberalism with a vision of politics that holds onto some version of rights, freedom, and equality. Some of these theorists, who are self-identified liberals like Will Kymlicka (1989), seem to assert that liberalism 'always already' encompasses ideals of relationship- and group-based identity central to feminism and socialism. Susan Okin's (1989) 'humanist liberalism' and Richard Dagger's (1997) 'republican liberalism' both seek to reread and reconfigure fundamental liberal features in ways that are more compatible with political theoretical ideals that are often seen as contradictory to liberalism. Even some socialist feminists have turned to liberalism in recent years. For instance, Susan Wendell's 'qualified defense of liberal feminism' ('qualified' by her preference for socialism) maintains that the individualism at the core of liberal feminism should be seen as utilising a more socially situated notion of the individual. Such an individualism would make 'liberal feminism ... a philosophically better kind of liberalism' (Wendell, 1987, p.66). Similarly, in her efforts to develop a 'liberal socialism', Chantal Mouffe reconfigures 'the individual ... as constituted by an ensemble of "subject positions", participating in a multiplicity of social relationships ... [and] a plurality of collective identifications' (Mouffe, 1993, p.85). Anne Phillips similarly links liberalism to socialism for feminist purposes, noting that 'Liberals have always insisted on the potential conflict between social equality and individual freedom; the difference with many contemporary socialists is increasingly a matter of degree.' (Phillips, 1993, p.41.) She particularly argues that feminists need to utilise the liberal category of 'rights', asserting that we need to expand our notion of what people have rights *to*, and that this requires us to 'shift the boundaries between what are public and what are private concerns' (Phillips, 1993, p.108) as has occurred in domestic violence, which is increasingly recognised as a crime and not a private, individual problem. In a different vein, feminist postmodern Drucilla Cornell (1995) does not mention the 'L-word' at all, yet has sought to redefine feminist politics in terms of what most would consider liberal rights, namely, rights to bodily integrity and 'the social conditions of self respect', which she explicitly draws from Rawls and Kant. Still others, such as Iris Young (1990), explicitly reject liberalism while unintentionally smuggling in liberal concepts such as 'rights' by the back door.

This ambivalence about liberalism suggests that we should view the relationship between feminism and liberalism as neither inherently contradictory (as socialist and radical feminists have argued in the past) nor as unproblematically consistent (as liberal feminists contend),[5] but rather as *paradoxical*. That is, we must simultaneously recognise that feminism *cannot exist* without certain key aspects of liberalism *and* that liberalism as it has been realised in most contemporary Western democracies is *premised* on women's inequality and unfreedom.

Recognising the paradoxical relationship between feminism and liberalism opens the door to rethinking that relationship, and redefining what is at stake in it. For instance, a key point of theories offered by Hobbes and Locke against patriarchal and divine right theories of political legitimacy in favour of a social contract model was to establish the importance of the *individual* as naturally free and equal, and therefore bound to political authority only by 'his' own individual consent. This argument was used by feminists such as Astell, Wollstonecraft, and Taylor to found modern feminism. But from a historical perspective, at least, it is clear that certain kinds of people (women, landless workers, and slaves) did not 'count' as individuals entitled to liberty and equality in most early liberal theories. As many feminists have argued, such exclusion should be seen as not just historically contingent, but necessary to the conceptual structure of liberalism (Di Stefano, 1991; Hirschmann, 1992; Pateman, 1988). That is, liberalism is not the innocent product of the social relations that 'happened' to predominate at the time; rather, those social relations importantly made possible, and were in turn made possible by, liberalism's (and capitalism's) emergence. Liberalism originated in, and has been at least in part built upon, a history of exclusion of women of all races and most classes, to varying degrees. In particular, what feminists have called the 'public/private split' developed in its peculiarly modern form out of the attempt to reconcile the somewhat contradictory forces of empowering the state to intervene in interpersonal relations when one individual violated the freedom of another and restricting the state from interfering uninvited. The point of government in the liberal view was to preserve and protect a robust 'private sphere' without, most emphatically, crossing the line *into* that sphere.

The family obviously fell under the 'private sphere', with the idea that interference in another's marital and parental relations was completely contradictory to notions of personal freedom: if individuals could not do what they wish in the privacy of their homes, they could do so nowhere. But such ideas did not apply to women, who were not considered agents able to make choices for themselves. Thus, under the rubric of 'privacy', women often suffered the abuse of their husbands and fathers with little recourse to political rights of state protection (Gordon, 1988; Brown, 1990). Though Mill (1992) argued repeatedly that such a state was a contradiction rather than an expression of liberalism, 'the individual' in liberal ideology appeared to be decidedly masculine.

This raises obvious dilemmas for feminists. If the liberal categories most central to modern feminism were developed by and through the ideological exclusion of women from those very same categories, then feminists interested in using 'rights' must acknowledge this historical indebtedness as well as the oppressive power these categories hold. Such an approach prevents us from saying that liberalism 'always already' contains feminist claims within its boundaries, that liberalism and feminism are unproblematically compatible. However, in contrast to those who reject liberalism altogether, it allows us to argue that such things as social individualism are *not inconsistent* with liberalism, that liberalism's premises of individual freedom and equality can be interpreted in such a way as to *allow* things like group rights. The idea that such notions are *required by* liberalism, that those who leave such notions out are simply incorrect, and even bad liberals, at the very least ignores the fact that the very first theorists we generally link with liberalism were themselves (despite their fairly consistent sexism, classism, and racism) diverse in their conceptions of the individual, definitions of freedom and equality, and prescriptions for political society. Such diversity suggests that liberalism is 'consistent with' a variety of different, even conflicting, notions and conceptions, *including* group rights and social individualism, but it also requires us to remember liberalism's abstract individualist heritage as well.

While such flexibility makes liberalism difficult to confront (indeed, a veritable moving target) and may even solidify its hegemonic grip on contemporary theory and politics, this flexibility is also what yields its feminist potential. Feminism compels us to recognise the racist, classist, and sexist history of liberalism: its initial institutional application only to propertied white men; its definitions of key concepts such as property and equality in ways that not only left out white women and people of colour, but depended on their subservience and classified them as forms of property; and its conceptualisation of individualism that ignored the importance of the relationship and connectedness that women's lives ensured.

At the same time, though, acknowledging such a history does not necessitate a *commitment* to its legacy. Concepts cannot be divorced from their historical foundations and development, nor can they declare total independence from their historical expression. But they are not inevitably proscribed by them either. Feminists must acknowledge the historical development and political-intellectual location of 'rights' through and in meanings and practices of racial, economic, and genderic exclusion and oppression. This acknowledgement, however, and perhaps paradoxically, allows us not to be locked into it. Indeed, it is only by attending to the history and foundation of liberalism that contemporary reconfigurations can occur with intellectual honesty. In the first place, critical acknowledgement of the racist and sexist foundations of rights allows us to see the self-contradictory elements within the concept. This, in turn, reveals how the structure of the framework within which rights were developed is antithetical to a feminist politics, for instance, by privileging white, middle-class women over poor women and women of colour. But it also requires us to recognise the ways in which feminism has emerged out of this framework – a recognition crucial to feminists' ability to evaluate our own potential inconsistencies and systematic exclusions – as well as to recognise the aspects of this otherwise undesirable framework that are vital to the attainment of a more consistent and more inclusive feminism. Indeed, perhaps it is significant that US feminists of colour such as Kimberle Crenshaw (1991) and Patricia Williams (1991), and international feminists such as participants in the UN conference on women (James, 1995), are holding onto and advocating the notion of rights, while those who tend to reject it are white, middle-class, Western academics.

It is by moving beyond – but not forgetting – such foundations through the particular configuration of its central ideals that feminism can access liberalism's political and philosophical power without being swallowed up by it. By admitting that 'liberal feminism' is self-contradictory, I want to suggest that feminists can, nevertheless, redefine the key terms of liberalism, particularly rights,without having to toss it aside as a relic of 'the dead white males'. By starting with feminist values, feminists can redefine and reshape the meaning of rights, rather than trying to adapt rights, as they have been historically constructed, to fit feminist goals. Obviously, this has its dangers; for the claim that a variety of ideas are 'not inconsistent with' rather than 'required by' liberalism means that each new interpretation is a redefinition and reconfiguration of liberalism; not the rediscovery of 'the truth', but an affirmation of and argument for particular *political* ideals.

That is to say, when reduced to its common denominators of 'individual freedom and equality', liberalism is a useful and attractive but nevertheless abstract and empty or 'open' term awaiting more particular (and political) definition and articulation by a certain kind of theoretical (and political) framework. As many have argued, liberalism as an ideology does not itself contain a particular politics. Rather, it is a *framework for* politics. This anti-political impulse of liberalism pervades liberal theory from Hobbes and Locke to Hayek (1960) and Nozick (1974), and operates on many levels, from liberalism's very foundation (an allegedly descriptive account of human nature that logically, even scientifically, derives forms of government from the 'facts' of human existence) to its institutional expression (the liberal ideal of the umpire state, refereeing differences in a pluralist society, but remaining by definition above the fray).

Feminists have argued that such so-called neutrality in fact contains a very specific politics, one that not coincidentally coheres with the interests of propertied white men, and this crucial observation has been the source of many feminists' rejection of liberalism. But this wholesale rejection does not force us to confront the real problem. And that is, by denying that they contain this politics, 'mainstream' liberal theories in effect erase their tacit modifiers: oppositional liberalisms, like welfare liberalism, become labelled, but other modifiers – such as white liberalism, patriarchal liberalism, or capitalist liberalism, each of which adapts the general liberal ideals of freedom and equality to specific political purposes, interests, and visions – are made invisible by appropriating the generic term 'liberalism'. This is where feminist criticism serves as a particularly useful analytical tool, however. If feminist critiques of 'liberal' theorists are correct (as I believe they are) that the ideals of freedom and equality are being used to advance the political power and agendas of particular groups, most often economically privileged white males, at the expense of other groups, usually white women, men and women of colour, and poor people of all races and genders, then to call such theory an unmodified 'liberalism', rather than, say, 'patriarchal liberalism' or 'white masculinist liberalism', involves the erasure of this political power and the denial of this agenda. Moreover, it is an erasure and denial so effective as to be hidden even from its very perpetrators, who, in circular fashion, are protected by the supposed 'neutrality' of their position from having to listen to feminist (and other) critiques at all. But just as a generalised 'feminism' often ends up really talking about white, Western, middle-class women (hooks, 1984), so is 'liberalism' often really talking about privileged, white, Western males.

As with feminism, however, this neutral facade for dominance does not mean that other groups cannot access its ideals. Hence, as an unmodified 'feminism' has given way to third-world feminism, Black US feminism, and lesbian feminism, to name just a few, there can be Black liberalism, socialist liberalism, or feminist liberalism, just as there can be patriarchal or capitalist or racist or white liberalism.[6] Such specifications and refinements reflect not essential being, but political positionalities; and liberalism, as a vague, but flexible, cluster of abstract concepts, can be tailored to a variety of experiences and needs, as the meaning of 'the individual' is particularised in those terms. By understanding liberalism in this way, the essence of the debate does not centre on liberalism *per se*, but rather on the various political positionalities attempting to lay claim to liberal ideals. The debate, then, should not be between feminism and liberalism, or even between different kinds of feminism, such as liberal and socialist, but between feminism and patriarchy, or white privilege and racial equality or capitalism and workers' control, each of which can adapt liberal ideals to its own ends. On this reading, liberalism merely provides the framework within which such political battles are carried out. It is in this sense that liberalism is 'neutral'; but such neutrality, precisely because it *is* open or empty, calls out for more particular content, a content that is provided by politics.

Rights Through Care

This is why I start off from Gilligan in my reformulation of rights. Obviously, Gilligan is far from a universal rallying point for feminists: she has been accused of racism and classism, as well as sexism insofar as her work is seen to reinscribe women in the traditional role of care-giver that many have blamed for women's subordination (Tronto,

1987). I have argued elsewhere why I believe that many of these criticisms are unjustified and misrepresent her argument (Hirschmann, 1992; see also Hekman, 1993), but my purpose in drawing on her here is only to *begin* a feminist conversation on reconceptualising rights, not to provide the final word. The general theme of 'care' that Gilligan introduced into the feminist vocabulary has been taken up by a variety of feminists, ranging from Nel Noddings (1984) (who takes an essentialist view of women as innately more caring because they are linked to biological processes of reproduction) to Nancy Chodorow (1978) (who locates care in the psychic reactions to the social relations of childrearing, such that women's raising children virtually ensures that girls will be more empathic and prone to caring activities, and boys will struggle to assert their separateness and individualism), to Sarah Ruddick (1989) and Nancy Hartsock (1984) (who each locate care not through essential emotions that all women feel, but in the material practices of mothering that most women perform, whether by choice or force), to Patricia Hill Collins (1989) (who argues that the practices of Black women's mothering have much greater capacity for an ethic of care than is true for either white women or Black men because race and class privilege distort that ethic). Care has been explored not only as a moral or ethical foundation, but as an epistemological framework (Belenky *et al.*, 1986; Hekman, 1993; Hirschmann, 1992) and a political value (Hirschmann, 1996; Mansbridge, 1996; Tronto, 1996).

Even so, it will undoubtedly strike many as ironic that I draw on Gilligan, since her 1982 book, *In A Different Voice*, has facilitated feminist analysis (including my own)[7] of the 'structural' sexism of liberal theory, and particularly of the problematically masculinist character of the notion of rights. In Gilligan's account of the classic Heinz dilemma developed by Lawrence Kohlberg (Heinz's wife is fatally ill and he cannot afford the medicine that will help her; should Heinz steal the drug?), the boy, Jake, responds that Heinz should steal the drug because 'life is worth more than money', in what Gilligan sees as a hierarchy of natural rights (Gilligan, 1982, p.26). The girl, Amy, by contrast, insists that the three people (Heinz, the druggist, *and* Heinz's wife) should talk the problem through and come up with another solution. Gilligan says that Amy's response embodies the care model, because it is based on face-to-face conversation, interpersonal dynamics, the centrality of relationship, and context, while Jake's rights-model response presupposes the breakdown (or even ultimate impossibility) of communication, a comparative assessment of property value (Heinz's wife versus the druggist's medicine or the money to be gained from its sale), and a hierarchy of rights which any rational person can see (a judge will give Heinz 'the lightest possible sentence' because stealing was 'the right thing to do' (Gilligan, 1982, p.29)).[8]

It is precisely this acontextual, abstract, mathematical, and impersonal picture of 'justice' that has caused rights to be eschewed by many feminists.[9] For as Elizabeth Schneider (1990, p.239) argues, 'Rights claims do not effectively challenge existing social structures,' and challenging and changing those structures is precisely what Heinz and his wife (not to mention feminists) need to do. But what this points to, I believe, is how in need we are of redefining and reconceiving rights in ways that accommodate the contextuality, constant change, need for flexibility, and dynamic interaction that characterises the care model.

Why a redefinition, however? Have not feminist lawyers made great strides in deploying traditional rights discourse to achieve important feminist goals such as access to abortion, protection of battered women, and sanction for sexual harassers? Certainly, I do not want to downplay this important work and the spaces it has opened up for feminists to redefine the political terrain. But there is obviously a certain circularity to the problem: how can women deploy rights if rights are defined so as not only to exclude them as rights-bearing *agents*, but to *include* them as subjects of *men's* rights claims? (Pateman, 1988.) Furthermore, how can women figure out what rights they want, how to define and articulate them, if their very subjectivity is constructed by and through a power structure that has their subordination at its core? (MacKinnon, 1987.) Certainly, it may be logical to assume that successes won by feminist lawyers deploying traditional rights arguments may, in turn, free women's imaginations and subjectivity so that we begin to envision ourselves differently, resulting in a further expansion of rights claims for women: the 'invention' of the notion of sexual harassment is a case in point. However, it is also the case that rights have been inadequate in tackling sexist barriers, because the framework in which they exist often cannot even see harm to women *as* harm, such as pornography, rape, or even sexual harassment. This is particularly the case in welfare, where the struggle to establish rights has simply failed (Bussiere, 1997). The traditional use of rights discourse ignores how the powerless are socially constructed not to want what the powerful does not wish to grant them. As Judith Butler notes, 'It is not enough to inquire into how women might become more fully represented in language and politics,' which is what a standard liberal rights approach does. Rather,

'Feminist critique ought also to understand how the category of "women", the subject of feminism, is produced and restrained by the very structures of power through which emancipation is sought.' (Butler, 1990, p.2.)

If Butler is correct, though, then why should feminists bother with the notion of rights at all? For starters, as Rachel Hare-Mustin and Jeanne Maracek (1990) argue about Gilligan's work, it may be that the voices of rights and care are not *gendered* voices at all, but rather voices of power and powerlessness; but if that is so, then perhaps the powerless need to access the voice of power. As Patricia Williams (1991) has argued, it is easy to talk about abandoning rights if you have been protected by them throughout your life; but for those who have been denied the protections that rights provide, giving up what they have never had merely furthers their disempowerment. Rights are powerful tools, Williams argues, so feminists should not be too quick to give them up. Frances Olsen (1984) similarly argues that because women have been denied rights throughout history, the argument that rights are bad because they isolate and disrupt community is simply not convincing, but only suggests the degree to which 'community' must be built on exclusion and subservience, a vision at odds with the care model. Similarly, Elizabeth Schneider (1990) maintains that in particular historical moments, rights have provided tools or weapons to the powerless to make claims to power, and through that to equality and democracy, whatever damage they may have also done.

But at the same time, that damage is fairly significant, and it is much more commonly the case that rights are used by the powerful to maintain their power. If rights are built upon assumptions of women's inferiority, but feminists want to hang onto them as an important strategy for obtaining equality, then rights need to be restructured from the bottom up. I believe Gilligan's care model suggests that this can be achieved in part by reconstructing rights along what might be called 'positive' lines that turn on the twin notions of responsibility she theorises. Certainly, the standard rights model has always contained within it a notion of responsibility: if I have a right to X, others have a parallel responsibility not to interfere with my pursuing X.[10] This notion of responsibility as 'negative' (as not doing what you might want to do because it would interfere with someone else's rights) involves refraining from actions that you would otherwise do but for the rights of others. The notion of rights requiring others' responsible self-restriction predominates in (patriarchal) liberalism, particularly as it developed in early social contract theory as a right to life and property, and later developed by Mill into rights of freedom of thought and self-regarding action more generally (see also Dworkin, 1977).

That is, the standard idea of rights-as-claims is 'negative': a right is a claim *against* someone else, a demand that they refrain from doing something they want to do because it interferes with something you want to do. Even in cases of apparently positive action, such as when courts order corporations to pay restitution to victims or to clean up pollution, rights are still based on a negative notion, because the real goal is to stop the corporation from doing what it did in the first place. By contrast, the notion of responsibility that Gilligan attributes to the care model is a 'positive' conception: rather than *not doing* what you would *otherwise do*, it involves *doing* what you might *not otherwise do*, taking positive action, as a means of providing care. An example might be what are sometimes called 'good Samaritan' laws, where someone observing a crime in progress who can act against it with little harm to herself (such as calling 911) has a positive responsibility to perform such action, because the victim of the crime has a 'right' to aid and assistance, as a form of care. Of course, the debates about such 'good Samaritan' laws involve a variety of complex issues that are not easily resolved. What constitutes 'danger' or 'little harm' to the self? How much is it reasonable to expect from bystanders or witnesses? Where does the line get drawn between responsibility and supererogation?

But that means that a positive vision of responsibility, not to mention of rights, would be more flexible, more contextual, and would proceed beyond the borders of 'individuals' as discrete entities to the communities within which individuals are situated and in which they were formed. It would attend to such social context both in terms of evaluating the *justification* of rights and of the *provision* of the right itself, so as to avoid unfair advantaging and the promulgation of inequality, which, in turn, would damage others' abilities to utilise rights. This would entail an explicit recognition of the social and political mechanisms that stand behind *all* exercises of even the most individualist liberal rights.

This 'positive' notion of responsibility, leading to a 'positive' conception of rights, is what makes me think that Gilligan's care model may be extremely helpful in reconfiguring rights. Gilligan's work has been drawn on by many feminists to set out a moral and political framework that attends to specificity, concreteness, and context which can provide feminism with important insights. Many non-feminist liberals complain that the major problem with taking a 'care conception' as a model of morality is that it violates the key liberal values of neutrality and universality, because it places such importance on relationship, and would therefore result in favouritism (Kohlberg, 1979; Rawls, 1971). To take an example, if my sister and I are in a prisoner-of-war camp where the water supply is minimal, and she is ill, care might seem to dictate that I figure out a way to sneak her an extra share of water. On the liberal view, this would violate other people's rights to an equal share of the water based on my subjective feelings of love and concern for my sister.

Such diametrical opposition between 'care' and 'rights' would seem to suggest that using Gilliganesque arguments to develop a feminist conception of rights is severely problematic. But I find it highly instructive and illuminating. For by using the care model as a *framework* for looking at liberal ideals – just as I earlier suggested that viewing liberalism as a framework for politics can liberate feminism to appropriate aspects of it to its own political agenda, as propertied white men have done – feminism can attend to both classical liberal notions, such as neutrality, *and* recent feminist arguments about the importance of relationship. That is, it can produce not just a 'blending' of the two, but a reformulation of liberal neutrality *through* relationally oriented feminist thinking. Such an approach can help us develop new concepts that cross the liberal/anti-liberal divide. For instance, I might make a plea to the other prisoners that those who need the water more desperately because of illness have a 'right' to a little extra because we all have an obligation to 'care' for each other.

This would be inconsistent with neutrality only if I cared exclusively for my sister and refused to honour other people's care claims, which is what liberals generally assume the 'care model' requires. But the ethic of care as Gilligan articulates it does not suggest such behaviour; care does result in 'partiality' in that it assesses needs and particularity and seeks to respond accordingly, but it does not mean that I give unfair advantage to those closest to me. Indeed, in Gilligan's treatment of the Heinz dilemma, Amy never suggests that Heinz should steal the drug because it is his wife (someone close to him, whose death would affect him personally) who is sick. This misattribution to Amy's motivation is common, but erroneous. Indeed, Amy says that Heinz should not steal the drug at all, which might seem to contradict typical understandings of the care model. Rather, Amy considers the needs of *everyone* involved; everyone is equally entitled to a prima facie consideration of care. It is only when details reveal greater or lesser need or ability that determinations of specific and appropriate expressions of care can be made. After all, we never know *why* the druggist will not give Heinz the drug. For instance, perhaps his child is also sick and he needs the money to care for her. Or perhaps his business is failing due to the recent competition of a huge chain outlet and with a large family economically dependent on him, he simply cannot afford not to be paid up front. Certainly, these may not be the case (the pharmacist may simply be greedy), but it is only by sitting down and talking the problem out as Amy prescribes, that such details can be articulated; and from such details can emerge a solution that expresses care for everyone. This represents a different notion of impartiality, one that is worked out through more knowledge rather than less, through concrete particularity rather than general abstraction, but it is impartiality nonetheless. Although it is no more foolproof than the standard rights model, it is also no less. Furthermore, it suggests that rather than opposing care to rights, a conception of rights can be developed *within* a care approach.

It also presents a strong notion of equality: by asserting the need to care for everyone, Amy is suggesting that everyone is of equal moral worth; Heinz's need is not necessarily greater because it is his wife who is dying, nor is the wife's need necessarily greatest because of her illness, nor is the pharmacist's property right. Certainly, the care model seeks to acknowledge the deep emotional attachments that relationships can give rise to, and, indeed, seeks to assert for them a role in moral discourse. But the point that Gilligan's theory makes is a methodological one: specifically, only through conversation among the three can an understanding of priority emerge, and such priority will not likely result in a zero-sum outcome. Rather, as Staughton Lynd (1984, p.1422) envisions, 'rights can be given a "positive sum" character, so that one person's exercise of a right enhances rather than diminishes another's'. In this, care operates from assumptions of equality; not necessarily that people are equal in their starting positions, but that equality of outcome is a goal to be worked for. Individuals should be given equal concern and respect, and their needs should be met equally, if that is possible. As William Simon explains in his vision of welfare rights, 'the autonomy of the claimant is a goal, rather than ... a premise of the system' (1985, p.16). As I have argued elsewhere (Hirschmann, 1992), the question in the standard rights model is 'whether' to act: Heinz, for instance, takes the mode of action (stealing the drug) as given, and considers *whether* to steal. Amy, however, addresses a different question, of 'how': what she takes as given is the need to care, and the question up for discussion is how to do that in a way that meets everyone's needs equitably and adequately.

The question of 'whether' is highly individualistic (I decide yes or no, do it or do not do it), but the question of 'how' is by definition a collective question because it involves communication so as to understand what different people need, and then working through possible alternative solutions.

This approach suggests that we view rights as a *social process* rather than 'things' or 'property' owned by individuals. The notion of 'conversation' is echoed by Elizabeth Schneider (1990) as an important element of this process of rights. Schneider argues for a 'dialectical' approach to the consideration of rights as abstract principles in terms of concrete political situations (such as welfare, or domestic violence, or rape) in order to allow feminists to be flexible and visionary in conceiving rights in new ways. Although for the most part she ends up only developing a strategy for changing the *content* of rights (that is, for making new kinds of claims for things that formerly had not been thought of as rights, such as a right not to be sexually harassed) and leaves the structure and meaning of rights (that is, as a 'claim against') pretty much intact, parts of her argument do seem to recognise the need to reconceptualise rights and gesture toward some useful ideas to that end. For instance, her conceiving of rights as a process of 'conversation' fits well with my notion of difference as an occasion, rather than a problem, for rights; if difference signals a time when rights need to be called into play, then engaging in conversation would seem an appropriate strategy for their invocation as well as for their definition. In other words, if 'difference' is to serve its purpose in rights, there must be avenues for rights claimants to be able to articulate their situation and their need, as well as their preferred solution. Individuals must be allowed and empowered to name their own experiences, and not have them named by others. We have all been parties to one-sided 'conversations' with overbearing colleagues or friends, and that is the only kind of 'conversation' possible under the current rights discourse: women are not only not allowed to tell their own stories, to express their needs in ways that will be listened to, but also the 'truth' of their experiences is told *for* them by those who have no knowledge of those experiences, and who distort them thereby, whether such distortions are well-intentioned but nevertheless ethnocentric or plainly misogynistic and racist, as we see today among social conservatives.[11]

As a *conversation*, however, it is not simply the responsibility of those in need to make such articulation. The standard, conflictual rights model leaves it to individuals to *assert* their rights, to yell loudly enough to be heard. But this simply perpetuates power inequality, for it is those whose 'differences' put them most in need of the protection that rights afford who are often least able to make such assertions. Rather, the notion of conversation requires the interaction of different individuals articulating their experiences, and at the same time not being hung out to dry because their lack of power has forestalled their ability to be heard.[12] Thus as William Simon suggests, rather than considering rights as 'trumps that ended conversations', they should be thought of as conversational tools that 'facilitated the beginning and middle as well as the conclusion of analysis'. In addition, rather than taking the identity and meaning of 'the individual' and 'the state' as each predetermined and given, he suggests, rights can and should be seen as 'an encounter between the individual [or groups of individuals, in keeping with his theme of the communitarian possibilities of rights] and the state in which the identity of each was partly up for grabs' (Simon, 1985, pp.15, 17).

Simon's approach, which he calls a 'social worker model', based on the philosophies and politics of progressive social workers at the turn of the century, does seem to cross over into romantic communitarian idealism at times, with its concurrent dangers of paternalism, but his remarks about the social constitution of the rights-bearing individual complements my own feminist reformulation of rights based on care. This approach avoids the reductive notion of a right as an antagonistic claim that asserts the inviolability of the separate individual and incorporates a notion that includes certain communitarian notions of individuals situated in relationships and contexts, as well as certain feminist elements of the importance of care as articulated by Carol Gilligan. Indeed, communitarian notions feed into and complement this vision, as Lynd (1984) reminds us, '"communal rights" are not the opposite of "individual rights"'. Rather, we need to see the 'communal content' in many individual rights, for instance, even the quintessentially individualist 'right to bear arms' depends on a global economy to provide guns and ammunition, a police force to distinguish between criminal and legal use of firearms (a distinction even the NRA is now acknowledging in Philadelphia, where it has committed substantial funds to the city to help to apply existing criminal law more effectively as a way to forestall new laws that would make the possession of firearms more difficult), as well as seeing yourself in relationship with others with responsibilities to them, so you can, for example, prevent your kids from blowing their heads off, not to mention killing their schoolmates.[13] Similarly, as Lynd suggests, even the right to free speech (another quintessentially individualist right) needs to be seen in terms of a social good. As Simon puts it, 'For the Progressives, the commitment to individual freedom and autonomy was a *social* commitment, and claims of right based on this commitment implicated collective concerns.... The enforcement of one person's rights is of concern to the others because it defines the society in which they all live.' (Simon, 1985, p.15.)

Rights, Difference, and Universalism: a Feminist Reframing

Rethinking rights through care also points the way to a more general reformulation of other liberal concepts and categories that are central to rights, through feminist attention to specificity and context. Thus, for instance, my approach suggests that feminists need not reject universality, as many feminists have argued, but rather that we can and should rethink universality along feminist lines. Ann Scales (1993), for instance, offers the term 'concrete universality' which (although she does not develop this concept in particular detail) is powerfully suggestive, for while the notion of universality allows feminists to acknowledge the similarities among women across race, class, and cultural lines, at the same time, viewing universality as 'concrete' forestalls its foundation in abstract beliefs about women's nature and requires that we base it on the material conditions of women's lives, the labour that they do, and the conditions of power in which they do it. It is derived from looking at women in various cultures and classes and seeing what is, rather than extrapolating grand theories of human nature from narrow culture- and time-specific samples. To this end, the proliferation of ethnographic studies and the production of feminist analyses by women throughout the world have enabled feminists to lay claim to liberal principles in a way perhaps not possible for white Westerners at the dawn of feminism's 'second wave' (see Moghaddam, 1994; Mohanty *et al.*, 1991).

Difference is thus vitally important to (my reading of) concrete universality, for it is only by understanding specific, concrete differences that the commonalities of gender oppression can be identified and theorised accurately. As Scales notes, 'concrete universalism takes differences to be constitutive of the universal itself' (Scales, 1993, p.101) in direct opposition to the dominant liberal rights vision of a universalism premised on sameness. Understanding differences between groups enables us to understand each other; and it is by understanding differences within our own groups that we can approach a more complete descriptive picture of them. Such completeness is necessary to any plausible conception of universality; the history of modern liberalism illustrates the ease and power of *falsely* universal claims, but it is only by gaining more complete pictures that we can approach valid claims of universality. Seyla Benhabib raises similar points in her arguments about the 'concrete other', an understanding of the other (similarly developed through Gilligan's work) as located in particular contexts and sets of relationships. The 'generalized other' that underwrites the abstract universalism of liberal rights operates from a 'vision of the self ... incompatible with the very criteria of reversibility and universalizability advocated by defenders of universalism.... Universality is not the ideal consensus of fictitiously defined selves' (whether in the state of nature or behind the veil of ignorance) 'but the concrete process in politics and morals of the struggle of concrete, embodied selves, striving for autonomy.' (Benhabib, 1987, p.81.) It is only by knowing as much as possible about the other – by knowing the other as concrete – that true reciprocity and reversibility, the hallmarks of liberal universalism, can be achieved.

Thus what concrete universality involves, to borrow from Chantal Mouffe, 'is not a rejection of universalism in favor of particularism but the need for a new relation of the two'. This new relation needs to allow for generalities and broad categories, which are necessary to the concept of 'human rights', but in a way that does not 'negate specific identities and repress specific communities' (Mouffe, 1993, p.85). Benhabib similarly argues for an 'interactive' notion of universality that acknowledges plurality without succumbing to relativism, that 'regards difference as a starting point for reflection and action' rather than as an answer (or rather, the non-answer of relativism) to moral dilemmas (Benhabib, 1987, p.81).[14]

Thus, concrete universality alters how we conceive of difference itself. Scales's notion of 'differences as systematically related to each other and ... as emergent, as always changing' (Scales, 1993, p.101) utilises the feminist commitment to particularity and difference to displace and transform the dominant (patriarchal) liberal push toward a basic sameness that underwrites its vision of rights. It thus helps reconfigure rights as things that *apply to individuals across differences*. That is, feminism recognises that 'individuals' exist in situated contexts, that they belong to various groups, that their 'individuality' is formed in part by virtue of membership in such groups; yet, *as* 'individuals', group membership does not contain the whole of their existence, and 'differences' exist not only between groups, but among individuals *within* groups as well. Thus, viewing difference as an *occasion* for rights – as a signal for when the protective power of the state may need to be called in – radically transforms the relationship between difference and rights, as well as difference and liberalism. For the responsibility of the state, through the invocation and enforcement of rights, serves not to erase difference, as has been the case in the past for white women and men and women of colour – who must either prove themselves 'the same' as white men, thus foregoing their specificity, or else hold onto their specificity and forego their rights – but to protect it. Viewing difference in this way allows liberal rhetoric to catch up with real social relations, in that claims of respect for 'difference' would be plausible, rather than serving as a cover for the privileging of a particular group.

Ironically, however, rather than reifying and essentialising difference, this focus on difference actually may reduce its substantive importance. That is, the relevant point becomes not whether women are, for instance, more caring than men, but rather whether such differences result in systematically unequal treatment and dominance. Feminism suggests a view of equality 'that focuses on the real issues [of *difference*] – domination, disadvantage and disempowerment – instead of on the interminable and diseased issue of *differences* between the sexes' (Scales, 1993, p.101, emphasis added). This suggests, in keeping with many feminist critics of liberalism, that we must be committed to equality of outcome and substance, rather than the (false) procedural equality typical of rights discourse. However, feminism does not require that we simply reject procedure. Rather, when equality of procedure produces inequality of outcome, the former has to be questioned as to whether it is truly 'impartial' or only facially, and misleadingly, so. Again, outcome, substance, and particularity become not so much ends in themselves, but rather become warning beacons to direct our theoretical and political attention to the possibility of power imbalances that have historically threatened liberalism and made it largely untenable for white women, men and women of colour, and the poor. Feminism should thus reject the opposition of procedure and substance found in many feminist critiques of liberalism. Yet feminism must draw on the insight inherent in such critiques (that procedures can appear to be neutral while perpetrating gross inequities) to help us create procedures that can attend to differences in context and situation, and are sensitive to substantive needs and outcome.

Conclusion

Thus what feminism needs to demand is a reconfiguration and specification of the general liberal notions of freedom, equality, universality, neutrality, individualism, and most importantly rights, in terms of feminist political values and goals. By starting with feminist values, feminists can redefine and reshape the meaning of liberalism and rights themselves, rather than trying to adapt them, as they have been historically constructed, to fit feminist goals. But since 'feminism', within the broad parameters I have sketched, embodies a broad range of specific political ideals and projects, many of them conflicting with one another, this may bring us full circle to ask: *which* 'feminist' ideals? That is one reason I began my reformulation from the work of Gilligan: she provides a starting point for defining *what* 'feminist political values and goals' are. Of course, not everyone agrees with her vision of 'feminism', but the unique advantage of using Gilligan is that since she is considered so directly opposed to rights, the ability to pull a rights argument out of her theory accomplishes what no other feminist framework can. This suggests, then, that my argument could serve as a kind of 'blueprint' which feminists of other persuasions could adapt to apply their own vision of 'feminist political values and goals' to the notion of 'rights' and 'liberalism' to similar effect. For instance, diverse political goals ranging from lesbian marriage (based on freedom of association and rights to privacy) to opposition to abortion (based on the argument that many abortions result from economic hardship and social stigma perpetrated by a sexist society, such that to talk of 'women's choice' is hypocritical at best) can be reconciled with the broad and generic 'liberal' outlines of individual freedom, equality, and rights (a right to marriage regardless of sexual preference and a right to have a baby without a husband, but without stigma, and under conditions of economic security) within recognisably feminist parameters.

Such parameters are crucial. Of course, for example, in contrast to the anti-abortion argument I just offered, which was based on *women's* rights to economic subsistence and freedom from sexist stigma, the more common pro-life argument for a 'right to life' for the 'unborn' could be legitimated through appeal to *liberal* ideals by couching its claims in terms of 'rights' for the foetus, but *not* to *feminist* ones, because foetuses take unilateral precedence over women in such a view. By contrast, the argument that abortion is wrong because women are destined by scripture to reproduce can be reconciled with *neither* liberalism *nor* feminism, and hence the language of 'rights' is not appropriate at all. Thus, the importance of feminist parameters lies in the recognition that not just anything can count as 'feminist'; but they also, nevertheless, suggest that feminism must accept as potentially legitimate a wider diversity of political views (such as opposition to abortion)[15] than are usually accepted as 'feminist'. Diversity among these specific political goals does not undermine feminism, but rather plays directly into it, as I have tried to show here: it is only by demonstrating respect and 'care' for difference that 'feminism' can hope to be inclusive of all 'women', but at the same time, it is by attending to difference that impartiality, universality, equality, and rights can be fully realised.

What this feminist approach to rights does is suggest a methodological shift in how we think, talk, and argue about rights, not to mention liberalism, a shift that brings politics to centre stage. But this emphasis on politics suggests that, in addition to rethinking liberalism and rights, we must also rethink difference, and I believe most feminists would agree with that; as I argued in the introductory section of this essay, the standard dichotomy between difference and equality within liberal discourse has always resulted in women having to assert *either* rights *or* gender and bodily specificity. But feminism can be true to itself only if it attends to both difference *and* rights; and in so doing, it can simultaneously break down some of the walls that have separated it from left-leaning 'mainstream' politics and theory for the past 30 years.

It is this overt emphasis on politics that highlights liberalism's flexibility, for by looking at liberalism as a more generic framework that can be *adapted by* various political positionalities, it is evident that this flexibility has good and bad effects, as I have argued: it can be used to patriarchal purposes as well as feminist ones. In this flexibility, however, lies the possibility that liberalism, formulated as a discourse to privilege a certain group of people, namely propertied white males, can be saved from itself by the very people it has historically excluded. As its critics, feminist and not, chastise a supposedly generic 'liberalism' for its hypocrisy and disingenuousness, we must remember what an important historical advance liberalism (even patriarchal liberalism) was, an advance that most likely made feminist and other left criticisms possible. In that paradox, a paradox that lies at the heart of the relationship between liberalism and feminism, also lies its power for transformation and endurance, a power which can well serve historically disempowered peoples.

ACKNOWLEDGEMENT

This paper was completed while an NEH-funded fellow at the Institute for Advanced Study in Princeton, NJ. Thanks to the Institute and to Cornell University for providing sabbatical leave and funding. Thanks also to Susan Hekman, Gordon Schochet, Michael Walzer, and several anonymous reviewers for their comments and suggestions. The faults that remain, of course, are mine alone.

NOTES

1. Since this is the third reference I have made to Flathman (1976) as an example of a classical liberal accounting of rights, I should acknowledge that his *The Practice of Rights* locates rights in social contexts of language and practices, even suggesting at times that rights might be somewhat context-bound and hence 'flexible' (for example, p.180), and thus seeks to avoid (and, indeed, hotly denies) the atomism that is often attributed to liberal accountings of rights (for example, p.185). But despite this, he does maintain rights as ruggedly individualist 'warrants' on other individuals or the state, or both, hence my references.
2. For critiques of the radical individualism of rights discourse, see Tushnet (1984), Lynd (1984), and Simon (1985). Even theorists who argue for a more 'communal' vision of liberalism maintain that individualism is its core value: as Norberto Bobbio observes, 'Without individualism, there can be no liberalism.' (Bobbio, 1990, p.9.) Theorists who tend to emphasise equality over freedom (as some suggest that Dworkin (1977) and Rawls (1971) do) emphasise equality among individuals, and for the purpose of the development of individuals rather than groups or classes. In this 'positive' or 'welfare' liberalism, states must take active roles in providing for the economic welfare of those at the bottom of the economic ladder as a way to equalise their freedom of choice to guide and direct their own lives as individuals entitled to 'equal respect'. But even Will Kymlicka, one of the leading contemporaries arguing for a liberalism that attends to the importance of group rights, maintains that 'Liberalism ... is characterized both by a certain kind of *individualism* – that is, individuals are viewed as the ultimate units of moral worth, as having moral standing as ends in themselves ... and by a certain kind of *egalitarianism* – that is, every individual has an equal moral status, and hence is to be treated as an equal by the government, with equal concern and respect.' (Kymlicka, 1989, p.140.)
3. See any number of feminist theory texts on liberal thought, such as Clark and Lange (1979), Di Stefano (1991), Hirschmann (1992), Jaggar (1983), Okin (1979), and Pateman (1988).
4. See, for instance, Pateman and Hirschmann (1991) about the difference between asserting the importance of 'freedom' as a *concept* and asserting the necessity of particular (liberal) *conceptions* of freedom.
5. See, for instance, Eisenstein (1981), Jaggar (1983), and Strossen (1995).
6. In *Liberal Racism*, Jim Sleeper argues that liberalism has promoted racism by exaggerating the effects of racial inequality and by lumping together all people of African descent as the same by virtue of their skin colour. While I find aspects of his argument extremely compelling, I believe, in fact, that he would be better off utilising the label 'racist liberalism', since he wants to acknowledge that many liberals do not promote racism, and that, indeed, 'liberalism' (a term he uses as a generic form) contradicts the uses to which it has been put by the individuals he criticises. See Sleeper (1997).
7. See Hirschmann, *Rethinking Obligation* (1992). I should note that some will undoubtedly read this paper as a retraction of my earlier work, but that would be to

misinterpret both my book and the present essay. For in *Rethinking Obligation*, I argued that obligation needed to be redefined away from a strict consensual model, that women's lived experiences of obligation as 'given' needed to be incorporated into public discourses and political theories. In addition, I argued that Gilligan's work highlighted important aspects of that experience. Thus obligation, which is seen in liberalism as a product of individualistic choice, had to be rethought through notions of connection, relationship, and positive responsibility. In the present essay, I am similarly making the case that rights, which are seen in liberalism as similarly individualistic and importantly related to choice and consent, need to be rethought in terms of care, connection, and positive responsibility. My critique of 'rights' in *Rethinking Obligation* was a critique of the classical liberal vision, but did not preclude the feminist rethinking of rights that I am engaged in here.

8. See Hekman (1993), Hirschmann (1992), and Tronto (1994) for fuller discussions of Gilligan.
9. Though many feminists believe that Gilligan's account seems to praise the care model as superior to the rights model, I agree with Susan Hekman (1993) that Gilligan does not really do so, but argues that justice and care are not only complementary, but interdependent, which is the part of her argument I am trying to amplify in this essay.
10. This could be called 'duty' by some political philosophers, which they would distinguish from 'responsibility'; see Hirschmann (1992), 'Introduction' and chapter two, for a discussion of why the language of 'duty' is both inappropriate and stacks the deck in such a way as to preclude the very kinds of questions that I believe a feminist consideration of 'responsibility' allows. Thanks to Gordon Schochet, however, for raising this question.
11. A good example of this kind of 'conversation' is when National Welfare Rights Organization lawyers in the 1960s (mostly white males) ignored NWRO members' (mostly African American single mothers) expressed desires to couch welfare rights in maternalist terms, and re-articulated their desire for rights in ways that the lawyers, not the women, wanted. See Bussiere (1997). See also White (1991), Crenshaw (1991).
12. On the importance of conversation between groups across differences within feminism, see Hirschmann (1998).
13. Though the NRA has begun an initiative in Philadelphia to help police enforce existing criminal laws involving the use of firearms more effectively, as a strategy to forestall more restrictive anti-gun legislation, it is much less amenable to the recognition of social responsibility. The infamous case of the deer hunter in New Hampshire who killed a woman in her own back yard, and based his legal defence on the fact that she wore white mittens which made her look like a deer, is a clear example of the ways in which rights could *not* be utilised under this formulation. A 'right' to use a gun would entail a much broader range of responsibilities than is currently the case, as I will argue below.
14. Although Benhabib's essay on 'the concrete and universal other' seems at times to treat 'concrete' and 'universal' as dichotomous terms, I read her use of concrete, like Scales's, as already attempting to mediate and reconcile the terms, rather than furthering the contrast.
15. The position articulated here, which I first encountered in a student paper on a political group called Feminists for Life, is not opposed to abortion *per se*, but rather to the social and economic conditions that often force abortion on women. The idea is that under current conditions, abortion is a violation of women's well-being. Presumably, if these conditions were changed (if there was wider access to contraception, if single motherhood was not stigmatised, and if the state provided adequate economic support for motherhood) abortions would likely decrease; but it

is less clear to me whether this position necessarily entails a moral opposition to abortion under any and all circumstances, as is the case with the other two 'right to life' positions outlined here. See Castonguay (1999)

REFERENCES

Astell, M. 1970. *A Serious Proposal to the Ladies*. New York, Source Book Press.

Belenky, M. F., Clinchy, B. M., Goldberger, N. R. and Tarule, J. M. 1986. *Women's Ways of Knowing: The Development of Self, Voice, and Mind*. New York, Basic Books.

Benhabib, S. 1987. The generalized and the concrete other: the Kohlberg-Gilligan controversy and feminist theory. In *Feminism as Critique*, ed. S. Benhabib and D. Cornell. Minneapolis, University of Minnesota Press.

Berlin, I. 1971. Two concepts of liberty. In *Four Essays on Liberty*, I. Berlin. New York, Oxford University Press.

Bobbio, N. 1990. *Liberalism and Democracy*. London, Verso.

Brown, G. 1990. Domestic Individualism: Imagining Self in Nineteenth-Century America. Berkeley, University of California.

Bussiere, E. 1997. *(Dis)Entitling the Poor: The Warren Court, Welfare Rights, and the American Political Tradition*. University Park (PA), Pennsylvania State University Press.

Butler, J. 1990. Gender Trouble: Feminism and the Subversion of Identity. New York, Routledge.

Castonguay, Kay 1999. Pro-life feminism. In *Feminist Philosophies*, ed. Janet A. Kourany, James Sterba and Rosemarie Tong. Second Edition. Upper Saddle River, NJ, Prentice Hill.

Chodorow, N. 1978. *The Reproduction of Mothering: Psychoanalysis and the Sociology of Gender*. Berkeley, University of California Press.

Clark, L. and Lange, L. 1979. *The Sexism of Social and Political Thought*. Toronto, University of Toronto Press.

Collins, P. H. 1989. *Black Feminist Thought: Knowledge, Consciousness, and the Politics of Empowerment*. Boston, Unwin Hyman.

Cornell, D. 1995. *The Imaginary Domain: Abortion, Pornography, and Sexual Harassment*. New York, Routledge.

Crenshaw, K. 1991. Mapping the margins: intersectionality, identity politics, and violence against women of color. *Stanford Law Review*, 43, July, pp.1241–99.

Dagger, R. 1997. *Civic Virtues: Rights, Citizenship, and Republican Liberalism*. New York, Oxford University Press.

Di Stefano, C. 1991. *Configurations of Masculinity*. Ithaca (NY), Cornell University Press.

Dworkin, R. 1977. *Taking Rights Seriously*. Cambridge, Harvard University Press.

Eisenstein, Z. 1981. *The Radical Future of Liberal Feminism*. New York, Longmans.

1989. *The Female Body and the Law*. Berkeley, University of California Press.

Flathman, Richard E. 1976. *The Practice of Rights*. Cambridge, Cambridge University Press.

Gilligan, C. 1982. *In A Different Voice: Psychological Theory and Women's Development*. Cambridge, Harvard University Press.

Gordon, L. 1988. *Heroes of Their Own Lives: The Politics and History of Family Violence*. New York, Viking.

Hare-Mustin, R. and Maracek, J. 1990. Beyond difference. In *Making a Difference: Psychology and the Construction of Gender*, ed. R. Hare-Mustin and J. Maracek. New Haven, Yale University Press.

Hartsock, N. 1984. *Money, Sex, and Power: Toward a Feminist Historical Materialism*. Boston, Northeastern University Press.

Hayek, F. A. 1960. *The Constitution of Liberty*. Chicago, University of Chicago Press.

Hekman, S. J. 1993. *Moral Voices, Moral Selves: Carol Gilligan and Feminist Moral Theory*. Cambridge, Polity Press.

Hirschmann, N. J. 1992. *Rethinking Obligation: A Feminist Method for Political Theory*. Ithaca (NY), Cornell University Press.

1996. Rethinking obligation for feminism. In *Revisioning the Political: Feminist Reconstructions of Traditional Concepts in Western Political Theory*, ed. N. J. Hirschmann and C. Di Stefano. Boulder, Westview Press.

1998. Eastern veiling, Western feminism, and the question of free agency. *Constellations: An International Journal of Critical and Democratic Theory*, Vol.5, No.3, September, pp.345–68.

Hobbes, T. 1968. *Leviathan*, ed. C. B. Macpherson. New York, Penguin.

hooks, b. 1984. *Feminist Theory: From Margin to Center*. Boston, South End Press.

James, S. 1995. U.N. treatment of multiple oppressions: a black feminist perspective. *Journal of African Policy Studies*, 1, winter, pp.53–69.

Jaggar, A. 1983. *Feminist Politics and Human Nature*. Totowa (NJ), Rowman and Allanheld.

Kohlberg, L. 1979. Justice as reversibility. In *Philosophy, Politics, and Society*, eds. P. Laslett and J. Fishkin. Fifth ser. Oxford, Blackwell Publishers.

Kymlicka, W. 1989. *Liberalism, Community, and Culture*. Oxford, Clarendon Press.

Locke, J. 1964. *Two Treatises of Government*. ed. P. Laslett. New York, New American Library.

Lynd, S. 1984. Communal rights. *Texas Law Review*, Vol.62, No.8, pp.1417–41.

MacKinnon, C. 1987. *Feminism Unmodified: Discourses on Life and Law*. Cambridge, Harvard University Press.

Mansbridge, J. 1996. Reconstructing democracy. In *Revisioning the Political: Feminist Reconstructions of Traditional Concepts in Western Political Theory*, eds. N. J. Hirschmann and C. Di Stefano. Boulder, Westview Press.

Mill, J. S. 1992. *On Liberty and Other Essays*. New York, Oxford University Press.

Moghaddam, V. M. 1994. *Identity Politics and Women: Cultural Reassertions and Feminisms in International Perspective*. ed. V. M. Moghaddam. Boulder, Westview Press.

Mohanty, C. T., Russo, A. and Torres, L. 1991. *Third World Women and the Politics of Feminism*. Indianapolis, Indiana University Press.

Mouffe, C. 1993. Toward a liberal socialism? *Dissent*, winter, pp.81–87.

Noddings, N. 1984. *Caring: A Feminine Approach to Ethics and Moral Education*. Berkeley, University of California Press.

Nozick, R. 1974. *Anarchy, State, and Utopia*. New York, Basic Books.

Okin, S. M. 1979. *Women in Western Political Thought*. Princeton, Princeton University Press.

1989. Humanist liberalism. In *Liberalism and the Moral Life*, ed. N. L. Rosenblum. Cambridge, Harvard University Press.

Olsen, F. 1984. Statutory rape: a feminist critique of rights analysis. *Texas Law Review*, Vol.63, No.3, November, pp.387–432.

Pateman, C. 1979. *The Problem of Political Obligation: A Critical Analysis of Liberal Theory*. New York, Wiley and Sons.

1988. *The Sexual Contract*. Stanford University.

Pateman, C. and Hirschmann, N. J. 1991. Freedom, feminism, and obligation. *The American Political Science Review*, 86, March, pp.179–88.

Phillips, A. 1993. *Democracy and Difference*. University Park (PA), Pennsylvania State University Press.

Rawls, J. 1971. *A Theory of Justice*. Cambridge, Harvard.

Ruddick, S. 1989. *Maternal Thinking: Toward a Politics of Peace. New York, Basic Books*.

Scales, A. C. 1993. The emergence of feminist jurisprudence: an essay. In *Feminist Jurisprudence*, ed. P. Smith. New York, Oxford University Press.

Schneider, E. 1990. The dialectic of rights and politics: perspectives from the women's movement. In *Women, the State, and Welfare*, ed. L. Gordon. Madison, University of Wisconsin Press.

Simon, W. 1985. The invention and reinvention of welfare rights. *Maryland Law Review*, 44, No.1, pp.1–37.

Sleeper, J. 1997. *Liberal Racism*. New York, Penguin Books.

Strossen, N. 1995. *Defending Pornography: Free Speech, Sex, and the Fight for Women's Rights*. New York, Scribner's.

Taylor, H. 1970. The enfranchisement of wsomen. In *Essays on Sex Equality*, ed. A. Rossi. Chicago, University of Chicago.

Tronto, J. 1987. Beyond gender difference to a theory of care. *Signs: A Journal of Women in Culture and Society*, Vol.12, pp.644–63.

1994. *Moral Boundaries: A Political Argument for an Ethic of Care*. New York, Routledge.

1996. Care as a political concept. In *Revisioning the Political: Feminist Reconstructions of Traditional Concepts in Western Political Theory*, eds. N. J. Hirschmann and C. Di Stefano. Boulder, Westview Press.

Tushnet, M. 1984. An essay on rights. *Texas Law Review*, Vol.62, No.8, May, pp.1363–403.

Wendell, S. 1987. A (qualified) defense of liberal feminism. *Hypatia*, 2, summer, pp.65–93.

White, L. 1991. Subordination, rhetorical survival skills, and Sunday shoes. In *Feminist Legal Theory: Readings in Law and Gender*, eds. K. T. Bartlett and R. Kennedy. Boulder, Westview Press.

Williams, P. 1991. *The Alchemy of Race and Rights: Diary of a Law Professor*. Cambridge, Harvard University Press.

Wollstonecraft, M. 1985. *A Vindication of the Rights of Woman*. New York, Viking Penguin.

Young, I. 1990. *Justice and the Politics of Difference*. Princeton, Princeton University Press.

3

Bodies, Passions and Citizenship

SHANE PHELAN

Discussions of identity and difference within feminist politics have centred on two lines of cleavage and connection. The first deals with the relation between men and women. Should the goal of feminist politics be for women to assert and achieve sameness with men, or should it be a recognition of women's distinctive, yet valuable, specificity? The second concerns relations among women. If we say that 'women' are either 'the same as' or 'different from' men, to which women (and which men) are we referring? It is clear that women differ among themselves as much as men differ from women.

The fact that the identity of 'woman' does not confer a single experience or consciousness may seem to pose a problem for feminism, inasmuch as feminism has been understood as a political position and analysis centred on women. And yet, this problem of identity has, instead, reinvigorated feminist theory. Problematising the figure of 'woman' has facilitated a renewed focus on gender and patriarchy as social structures affecting everyone. The political goal of equality for women cannot be achieved without thorough examination of the structures of thought and society that have made political equality seem scandalous. The theoretical task of feminism is not to look at women in isolation from or in opposition to men, not to derive general principles concerning women, but is to demonstrate and deconstruct the pervasive masculinisms of historical and contemporary cultures. To be sure, these masculinisms are variable as well, and we need not derive an ideal type of masculinism in order to understand particular forms and manifestations. Grasping particular masculinist formations and the ways in which women and other 'others' are excluded through them will enable us to understand better what sorts of political action are needed in particular locales.

In order to show how masculinist conceptions of bodies and passions work to exclude 'others' from equal citizenship, I will examine the ideal of the phallic citizen body and the trope of the body politic in public discourse in the USA. Focusing on civil rights and membership, I will argue that objections to the equal citizenship of lesbians, gays, bisexuals, and transgendered people are constituted and articulated through concerns for the integrity of the heterosexual masculine political body. My paper proceeds in several stages. In the first part, I survey the connection between the normatively white male citizen body and the exclusion of those whose bodies do not 'fit'. I present phallic masculinity as one mode of masculinity that has implications both for the exclusion of particular individuals and for the figuring of the body politic as a whole. In the second section, I turn to the role of passion in liberal and republican discourse. Most feminist scholarship has focused on the liberal 'man of reason' to argue that phallic masculinity demands the absence of passion. The republican tradition, however, insists on passions, albeit particular, 'manly' passions. A brief treatment of the labouring citizen body and the role of sexual renunciation completes my survey of phallic masculinity. In the fourth section, I discuss how phallic understandings of agency in general have shaped discourses of civil rights in the USA. In the final section, I turn to the body politic and the threat posed by non-normative sexualities. I argue that attempts to bypass republican themes in favour of a liberal discourse of inclusion are doomed to failure. Republican discourse remains an important element of American political thought, and its figurations of passion, citizen bodies, and the body politic must be confronted directly if sexual minorities hope to change attitudes and policies.

Citizen Bodies

Masculinisms function by promoting certain characteristics as 'masculine' and making those characteristics the criteria for full membership in polities and societies. It is not the construction of masculinity that excludes and oppresses, but the ways in which masculinity becomes a privileged mode of being. These constructions not only figure women as other, but also produce difference itself as feminine. Thus, those women and men who are seen as other become 'feminised' in various ways, treated as the other of whatever masculine ideal prevails in a given society.

Cultural conceptions of bodies have been among the major vehicles of masculinism in the West. Understandings of the required features of the citizen's body, imbricated with cultural conceptions about various sorts of bodies, have worked to exclude from citizenship the majority of the population of most Western nations. Through metaphors of the body politic, cultural conceptions about physical bodies migrate as well into rhetoric and policy about the nation-state. These rhetorics express and construct new opportunities and threats to political units, including states, nations, and social movements. The trope of the body structures concerns for (among others) integration, boundaries, power, autonomy, freedom, and order; as Catherine Waldby explains, 'a shared set of corporeal metaphors are drawn upon to imagine the conditions of unity and integrity for both the social field and the particular body, and in the process to reconcile the one to the other' (1996, p.89). Thus, the idea of the body works both to delineate who shall be a member of the polity and to prescribe the nature of the polity itself.

Some theorists have found the body politic to be a positive and fruitful concept. John O'Neill, for example, argues that the body politic 'is the fundamental structure of our political life. It provides the ultimate grounds of appeal in times of institutional crisis, hunger and alienation, when there is need to renew the primary bonds of political authority and social consensus.' (O'Neill, 1985, p.77.) O'Neill's concern for the rise of technocratic/administrative logics leads him to celebrate 'anthropomorphism and familism' as 'the root values of political discourse seeking to correct the excesses of neo-individualism and statism' (1985, p.83). Others, such as Waldby, have pointed out that the other side of the body politic's bonding function is the delegitimation of that which is excluded from current social consensus. The role that O'Neill finds so reassuring is exactly the one that others fear.

Tropes of the body allow for particularly powerful migrations of concerns about gender and sexuality into political discourse (Waldby, 1996, p.89; Schatzki and Natter, 1996). These concerns emerge in foreign policy as well as in legislation on health and welfare, immigration, regulation of the media, education, and family policy. Fear of chaos and disorder, of sexual predation, of the loss of control meet the desire to transgress prohibitions and reach beyond the given on the many terrains of political action.

The predominant critical account of the relation between bodies and citizenship has been produced in feminist critiques of Western philosophy (Bordo, 1993; Butler, 1990). These critiques have suggested that the body of the citizen is not only normatively male, it is invisible. The opposition male/female is linked to mind/body, and citizens as rational beings are construed not only as male, but as characterised only incidentally by bodies (though curiously, it is their body that tells us in daily life that they belong to the class of persons for whom bodies are secondary). A variant of this position does not deny that men have bodies, but it denies that they *are* bodies. The contrast between male and female is not between embodied beings and disembodied minds, but rather ranks how much that embodiment affects their lives. Male bodies are containers for minds that guide bodies, while female bodies overwhelm their minds.

This analysis must, of course, be modified by several other factors to be useful. Not all male bodies count as appropriate citizen bodies; in Western society, non-white men are more fully embodied than white men, workers are more embodied than middle-class men, and gay men are so completely embodied as to threaten civilisation itself. When women or any of these 'others' appear in public, they emerge with what Lauren Berlant has labelled as 'surplus corporeality' (1997, p.178). This is the result of their inevitable difference from the white male norm, a norm that not only never needs saying, but is actively threatened by some forms of saying. As Berlant notes, 'the power to suppress that body, to cover its tracks and its traces, is the real sign of authority' (1997, p.176; compare Bordo, 1997).

This account serves to explain not only the rejection of women's bodies, but also the ways in which women and people of colour are specified as exceptions to the 'generic' category of citizenship. The particularity of bodies not white, male, and heterosexual qualifies claims to a citizenship that is putatively universal. As the most universal of categories within a nation-state, citizenship seems to be among the most solid strongholds for the unmarked universal. Those whose citizenship is qualified by distinguishing features are never as completely citizens as those whose identities seem to offer no intermediate, potentially conflicting, affiliations.

Recent queer and feminist work, however, has expanded on the idea of the citizen body to suggest that the normative male body is not absent from public view, as it so often is in philosophical texts, but emerges as phallic. The phallic body is impermeable, a source but never a receptacle. Such a conception works within a chain of associations that link personal receptivity, vulnerability, fluidity, and disintegration of the self (Irigaray, 1985). Thus, as Anthony Easthope tells us, 'the most important meanings that can attach to the idea of the masculine body are unity and permanence' (p.53). This stability is both physical and mental. In this view, men, guided by inner imperatives and directed by reason, find their goals and their way without deviating. The phallic ideal of the body is also manifested in the masculine denial of physical pain and in the suspicion and disdain shown to men who notice and fashion their bodies. Each of these gendered associations plays off the idea that masculine bodies and minds are fixed, stable, self-maintaining, and invulnerable.

In sharp contrast, feminine bodies are 'castrated', incomplete, and vulnerable. Their distance from the signifier of strength and purpose leaves them weak in both body and mind. This is evident in a myriad of daily associations. Note, for example, the popular saying that changing one's mind is 'a woman's prerogative', but not a man's. Women are fickle, both in thoughts and desires, and must be tolerated by men (who, of course, know their own minds and so do not change). This is consistent with women's fuller embodiment and their consequent susceptibility to the change that is part of the phenomenal world.

This difference in bodily construction is not incidental to larger social arrangements. As Elizabeth Grosz has argued, 'patriarchy is psychically produced [through] the constitution of women's bodies as lacking' (1994, p.60). Convincing both men and women that women's bodies are lacking is a cultural project; while boys may understandably see women's bodies as missing what they possess, girls require a more extensive shift. Further linking bodily difference to qualities of mind is essential to representing men as powerful and privileged; in Grosz's phrasing, 'if women do not lack in any ontological sense (there is no lack in the real, as Lacan is fond of saying), men cannot be said to have'. Masculinity can be phallic only because femininity is vulnerable, castrated, and unfixed.

This oppositional dependence means that the phallic position is continually a position full of anxiety. The project of being a phallic subject always contains the threat of being overcome by that which it excludes; the phallic subject always runs the risk of being exposed as needy and incomplete. In Susan Bordo's observation, 'actual men are not timeless symbolic constructs; they are biologically, historically, and experientially embodied beings; the singular, constant, transcendent rule of the phallus is continually challenged by this embodiment' (Bordo, 1997, pp.31–2). Thus, the phallic, self-contained subject inevitably generates its own outside, an outside that threatens to unmask actual men as impostors. The vulnerability of actual bodies, both male and female, threatens men with the removal of authority.

Many, if not most, bodies cannot aspire to full phallic status. Some suffer from femininity, others from a hypermasculinity that is inconsistent with liberal citizenship. Feminine bodies, whether female or male, are those that 'leak' across the boundaries of the phallic imagination. Such bodies may literally leak, as in menstruation, or they may allow for receptivity and thus be 'passive', vulnerable to others. In either case, they are understood to present incomplete boundaries and thus represent the possibility of threats to the masculine self. In Elizabeth Grosz's words, 'in the West, in our time, the female body has been constructed not only as a lack or absence but with more complexity, as a leaking, uncontrollable, seeping liquid; as formless flow; as viscosity, entrapping, secreting; as lacking not so much or simply the phallus but self-containment – not a cracked or porous vessel, like a leaking ship, but a formlessness that engulfs all form, a disorder than threatens all order' (1994, p.203). Such a being must be subordinated in order for the phallic self to avoid being overcome.

The hypermasculine body, such as the body of the slave or his sons, is too much body rather than a leaky one. It threatens the masculine body even as it seems to exemplify it. The hypermasculine body is the result of too much corporeality and not enough time in an armchair. The exposure of the hypermasculine body leads to its emasculation, rather than its feminisation. By this I mean to refer to the loss of authority consequent on 'too much' embodiment. Although Black athletes in the USA are exemplars of one form of masculinity, it is not a form that carries cultural authority or that increases the power of Black people in general (Connell, 1995). In fact, as Bordo notes, racist discourses that force Black men 'to carry the shadow of instinct, of unconscious urge, of the body itself – and hence of the penis-as-animal, powerful and exciting by virtue of brute strength and size, but devoid of phallic will and conscious control' serve not to enhance respect and authority but to undermine it (1997, p.37). Similarly, the hypermasculinity of some gay men serves to open them to violence and hatred rather than inclusion. Phallic masculinity is characterised by initiative and activity, but also by self-control. Exposure of too much of the male body, or of finely honed male bodies, may draw some admiring looks, but works to disqualify one from liberal citizenship. The fiction that the male body is not really a body is belied not only by men who craft their bodies, but also by men who use them 'too much', whether in work or in swagger or in violence.

This 'imaginary anatomy', in Lacan's phrasing, has profound

implications for politics. The quintessential capacities of the modern citizen, autonomy and self-control, are associated with the limited embodiment of the masculine self. These capacities are then conferred upon those whose actual anatomy is seen to accord with it. The liberal citizen is normatively not only male, but masculine, white, and heterosexual. Not only is the citizen delineated by race, gender, and sexuality, but the body politic as a whole shares the attributes of the citizen. The imaginary anatomy of the body politic is masculine, and it serves to exclude, in Moira Gatens' phrase, 'those whose corporeal specificity marks them as inappropriate analogues to the body politic' (1991, p.82). The exclusion of 'others' is not a function of their corporeality alone, but of the wrong corporeality: on the one hand, a corporeality that opens them to others and potentially subjects them to another's will, on the other, a mode of embodiment that threatens the phallic citizen.

Political Passions

Although liberal theories have trouble with embodiment, they do by and large recognise passion. Passions seem to be features of minds that have no clear connection to bodies. Bodies appear in liberal theory as vulnerable: to pain, to hunger and cold, and to attack. This presentation is indebted to a Stoic-inflected Christianity in its asceticism. Liberal theory evokes threats to the body, challenging phallic masculinity, in order to suggest schemes of rescue. The ideal of ordered liberty requires bodily comfort, but liberals disagree on whether this is the ultimate goal of politics. For Locke and Hobbes, physical security seems to be the main virtue of civil society. For Rousseau and Kant, however, the goal of government was the establishment of autonomy among citizens. For all of these theorists, passions tell us about our particular desires, but they are not to be followed. Rather, Hobbes and Locke hope to substitute interest for passion, precisely because it is more stable and permanent. Reason follows interest and constrains passion.

Among the passions to be disciplined is love. Love is not to be eliminated, but it is to be relegated to 'private' life, specifically the family. Love binds, but also inspires conflict; in either case, it is too particularistic for politics. Liberal theorists have no room for love, just as they have none for hatred or any other disruptive passion. The goal of liberal politics is not to build relations of sympathy or solidarity, nor to rely on them, but rather to make the world safe for masculine bodies.

Speaking of the tradition of contract theory, Carole Pateman has noted that the classic texts tell us that women 'cannot transcend their bodily natures and sexual passions': 'Women's bodies symbolize everything opposed to political order.' (Pateman, 1989, p.4.) For the contract tradition, with its concern to replace or moderate passion with reason, women's exclusion has been justified by their inability to control themselves.

Although Pateman's analysis of the exclusion of emotion and bodies applies to liberal theory, however, it is less satisfactory for understanding republicanism. Both liberal and the republican bodies are phallic in their impermeability and autonomy, but they have quite different relations to citizen bodies and to the passions. Discerning this difference offers us a more nuanced portrait of contemporary American citizenship than that afforded by critics of liberalism alone. Passions are important for liberals, but are to be removed from the public sphere as much as possible. For civic republicans, on the other hand, love and hate are the foundations of polities. As Hannah Pitkin describes Machiavelli's view, 'the city is a woman and the citizens are her lovers' (1984, p.26), or, in the words of Pericles, citizens should 'gaze, day after day, upon the power of the city, and become her lovers' (Thucydides, II.43.1). This view appears in a number of permutations, most prominently in times of war. Whether motherland, fatherland, or simply Uncle Sam, the polity figured in republican rhetoric is an object of adoration and devotion and the citizens are children who must fight to protect the threatened parent.

The most important republican passion is love: for one's country, for its laws, and for one's fellow citizens. This love is an important contrast to the liberal who is either passionless (in the Kantian and Rawlsian models) or whose passion is in need of subduing (Hobbes and Locke). Summarising Machiavelli's view, Pitkin notes that 'without passion and struggle, there can be no liberty, but only reification, habit, and drift' (1984, p.300). This passion is both a love for one's country and love for one's countrymen, the fellow sons of the city.

Republican love, however, is narrowly bounded. It is a love simultaneously personal and abstract, in which others are loved as citizens, but not as individuals. Citizens are not loved by other citizens because of their personal virtues or qualities, but because they are fellow citizens. The primary love is for one's country; love of one's fellow citizens flows, as it were, in a circuit from citizen to country to citizen, much as Christians are held to love one another through their love of Christ. The republican's love is intense, allowing for self-sacrifice even to death, but it is not a love of persons, but of the idea of persons, or of the country as a person.

This intense yet abstract love is curiously similar to certain formations of phallic masculinity. What earlier feminist theorists labelled 'abstract masculinity', in which masculinity derives its content solely from its contrast to femininity (compare Hartsock, 1983), has a political corollary in republican citizenship. Republican citizens do not love their country completely abstractly; most writers agree on the importance of particular geography and national features to the love of one's country. But the love of one's fellow citizens, which must be abstract given that one cannot know them all, much less love them all, is rather a love for the idea of one's fellow citizens. It is not a particular, but a universal love – a curious blend.

One of the primary threats to such citizenly love is the particular love for another, especially romantic love. From Aristotle to Machiavelli to Rousseau, and latent in today's controversies over queer citizenship, we find the concern that romantic love's 'particularising' force has the potential to destroy polities. There are several reasons for this power. First, romantic love makes for preferences among citizens. Such preferences may lead one to neglect one's civic duty in order to protect or privilege loved ones. Second, romantic love creates conflicts. Among heterosexual men, these conflicts are between men for a particular woman, and within each man as he wrestles between civic and romantic love. Romantic love has the potential for neglect of duty and for internal division as men love women over their country.

Most republican theorists and politicians have resolved this problem by privatising women so that each man emerges in the public world as 'citizen x' rather than 'Joe who got my girl'. They seek not to eliminate romantic love, but to wall it off. Controlling women is a crucial element of what Carole Pateman (1988) has described as 'fraternal patriarchy'. Such control is not unique to republicanism; indeed, Pateman's focus is on liberal theory. As she notes, however, the liberal citizen is defined 'in opposition to the political and the masculine passions' that are central to republican understandings. The republican fraternal contract does not require the elimination of such passions, but constrains their disruptive effects by controlling women. Thus, the good republican society requires sharp sexual differentiation and separation in order to allow for the mutual dependence of free men. Homosocial passions are not only safe in such a society, they are required as an element of fraternity. Their free flow depends upon a pattern of simultaneous acknowledgement and denial: acknowledgement of their fraternal love and commitment with denial of any sexual or erotic elements.

A recognition, even an embrace, of passion should not be mistaken for an idealisation of a less phallic body. The passionate citizen is inner-directed, with passions moving outward toward others but never being penetrated by fashion or the whims of others. The focus on discipline is not a denial of passion, but urges its channelling from formlessness to phallic ordering. Through their love of the city, citizens conceive themselves as simultaneously passionate and controlled. One does not demonstrate manly virtue by lack of passion, but through conquering it, manifesting one's strength (Monoson, 1994).

In David Halperin's treatment of the Athenian citizen body, he argues that democracy produced 'a new kind of body – a free, autonomous, and inviolable body undifferentiated by distinctions of wealth, class, or status: a democratic body, the site and guarantee of personal and political independence' (1990, p.98). Political equality was premised on the self-understandings of male citizens as 'lords over their own bodies' (Halperin, 1990, p.99), in contrast to all those who lacked such authority: women, slaves, children, and foreigners. Although 'homosexuality' was acceptable, adult male citizens were enjoined to participate only as penetrators. Allowing oneself to be penetrated, then as now, was evidence of one's unfitness for equality. It must be noted that the failure was not of excessive passion, for the *eromenos* was not seen as passionate, but rather of a willingness to be receptive. The passionate citizen was crucial to the welfare of the polity, but the passions must be 'manly' ones.

Both Monoson and Pitkin note the importance of mutuality in this understanding. Because citizens cannot be subordinate or submissive to others, both the Periclean and the Machiavellian versions of republicanism work to provide a vision of connection that does not violate the phallic conception of the citizen. Thus, both suggest that politics is not a matter of domination of fellow citizens, but is a relationship among manly peers; those who can be dominated do not belong. This vision of mutuality, however, is constantly interrupted. Eros is continually figured for Machiavelli in terms of domination and possession (Pitkin, 1984, pp.25, 301). The full mutuality of citizens that is evoked in republican literature is interwoven with images of threat and contest. Love of the polity does not mean submission to it, or even respectful consideration of the many persons in it, but, instead, legitimates domination in the name of the saviour. As lovers of the city, citizens may decide what the beloved shall do and be.

War is a prominent but not the only scene that calls forth such passionate images. In general, for republicans passion and struggle are the means to ensure freedom. Complacency is the greatest danger to republics. From Pericles to Theodore Roosevelt, republican politicians have excoriated complacency and narrow self-interest. The author of the Cato letters in eighteenth-century America wrote that 'virtue is the passion for pursuing the public good, with which the lesser passions may compete, but into which they may equally be transformed' (Pocock, 1975, p.472). The public realm is, in his understanding, 'a device or mechanism for requiring men ... to erect an edifice of reason and virtue on a foundation of passion' (Pocock, 1975, p.472). A century later, Roosevelt stressed that the character of a citizen must combine 'resolution, courage, energy, power of self-control, combined with fearlessness in taking the initiative and assuming responsibility' (Pocock, 1975, p.3). Indeed, for Roosevelt 'the democratic ideal must be that of subordinating chaos to order' (Pocock, 1975, p.12). The goal of education for citizenship is to produce men who can see the good, desire it, and will its enactment. His stress on discipline and obedience to the law recalls Abraham Lincoln's exhortations to obey the law, exhortations rooted in a keen appreciation for the vitality and the volatility of passion (Lincoln, 1992, pp.16–19).

This ideal is deeply imbricated with cultural conceptions of gender. The American Revolutionary generation explicitly maintained the republican dichotomies of independence/dependence, constancy/fickleness, and control/licence as measures not only of women's distance from men, but also of the failings of individual men. This was not incidental to their project, as Linda Kerber notes, among that generation, as for earlier and later republicans, 'anxieties for the stability of their construction led them, as they emphasized its reasonableness, its solidity, its link to classical models, also to emphasize its manliness and its freedom from effeminacy. The construction of the autonomous, patriotic male citizen required that the traditional identification of women with unreliability, unpredictability, and lust be emphasized.' (Kerber, 1997, p.264.)

Kerber points out that these associations run throughout the twentieth century as well, as manifested in university curricula in 'American civilisation' (1997, p.221). The distinction between manly and 'weak' passions continues today, sometimes under the code of 'will' versus 'emotion'. Those who display vulnerability directly, through tears or the expression of compassion, are 'emotional'; those otherwise rational men who exhibit anger or frustration are 'strong' or 'forceful'. Now, sometimes those who manifest anger or frustration are not authorised to do so, by virtue of their embodied status. When they do so manifest, they are emotional rather than forceful. We cannot say simply that some passions are manly and others are not. We must look at who is displaying them, how, and for what cause. When Madeline Albright, Clinton's Secretary of State, shows anger with Saddam Hussein she is strong; were she to display such vehemence concerning women's oppression or on behalf of queer equality, I suspect she would be seen as hysterical.

Women can, nonetheless, have civic passion in republican theory. Although they are not to be direct combatants, women's role as mothers and their extension of that role to support of the body politic requires passionate love of their country. It is not the amount of passion that disqualifies women from full citizenship, but the nature of their passion (fickle and inconstant) and their inability to control themselves. The body politic requires the support of those who can be counted upon to defend it with their lives.

Labouring Citizens

American citizenship is no longer measured simply by the republican criteria of bearing arms, voting, and concern for public honour. The social standing central to citizenship is found before the law and in politics, to be sure, but more importantly it is to be found in 'the marketplace, in production and commerce, in the world of work in all its forms, and in voluntary associations' (Shklar, 1991, p.63). Here is where a citizen finds 'his social place, his standing, the approbation of his fellows, and possibly some of his self-respect' (Shklar, 1991, p.63). In this context, not working amounts to the loss of public presence as well as approval. Those who do not work cannot be independent, and if they are not independent, they are not only less than equal, they are a drain on those who work. In contemporary American society, the threat of luxury and corruption so central to republican rhetoric bears the faces of welfare mothers, slackers, and immigrants (as well as sexual minorities, for reasons we will see shortly).

The peculiar importance of work, Shklar argues, arises from the centrality of the contrast between free and slave in US history. The 'American work ethic' she describes as 'the ideology of citizens caught between racist slavery and aristocratic pretensions', an ideology that has endured because the political conditions to which it responded from the first have not disappeared' (Shklar, 1991, p.64). The phallic binary of agent/slave may have its roots in this unique situation. The stark division between free and slave has always been a resonant and overused part of American political language.

The fetishisation of labour has perpetuated the myth of phallic agency. The labouring body endures; it is disciplined; it is productive. In the USA, the labouring body is the citizen body. Bodies that fail identification with the labouring body must be suspect as citizen bodies. Not all citizen bodies labour, of course, but the citizen ideal in the USA labours in the market. The individual who is cared for by others (whether by family members or the state) is not considered a worker, and thus does not present herself as a citizen (Fraser and Gordon, 1994; Pateman, 1989, pp.179–209; Young, 1997, Ch.6). Her body is not seen as a labouring body, because its labour is invisible to the market. Women's campaigns for access to work relied on this point, treating work as the precondition of effective citizenship. This ideal of labour has limited the progress of social rights in the USA. Not only are women who do not earn treated as less than equal, their homes and bodies open for state inspection, men who fail to produce are often denied even the minimal welfare allotted to women and children. The ideology of phallic masculinity mandates that any man worth his citizenship be a worker. The absence of welfare, training programmes, and other social support for single men signals a widespread willingness to deny acknowledgement to those who do not act like 'real men'.

The ideology of labour should not obscure the fact that late capitalism thrives on producing consumers rather than workers. The actual situation of the contemporary USA is much more complex than the ideology of labour suggests. In fact, one of the things that native Americans find 'strange' about immigrants is their willingness to labour, whether at school or at work. Nonetheless, the ideology maintains labour as a crucial part of American identity and a central rhetorical figure in public policy debates (see, for example, Galston, 1991).

The association of citizenship and labour suggests a fruitful avenue for understanding the position of lesbian, gay, bisexual, and transgendered people. The sexual body invoked by gay, lesbian, and queer political campaigns directly challenges the working body of the labouring citizen. Citizenship and labour both require discipline and renunciation. Although campaigns for equality do not emphasise sexual practice, the very identity that is stigmatised invokes sexual desire and the promise of pleasure; furthermore, the heavy focus within these debates on gay men and the fact that men are the primary policy and opinion makers means that those most directly governed by the ideology of phallic masculinity are being haunted by their other. Pleasure, present in republican thought only as luxury and corruption, is trying to work its way into citizen bodies. Thus, campaigns for sexual equality run directly counter to both liberal disembodiment and republican phallicism.

Which sexual renunciations are called for in order to become citizens? More directly, what is the status of work that mixes labour and sex? The contradictions faced by sex workers, legal and illegal, are profound. Free labour has been one of the great integrating forces in the USA, as immigrants earned respect through work. Civil rights, beginning with the right to settle in the USA, have often hinged on one's status as an employable worker. On the other hand, the manifestation of sexuality (other than working-class white masculinity) has been considered a disqualification for full membership. Those who cannot or will not isolate their sexual bodies from their working bodies pose a major challenge to the theory and practice of citizenship.

Phallic Agency and Civil Rights

Under the pressure of feminist movements, the earlier explicit exclusion of women from political membership has been attenuated. Women in the USA today are accorded many (though not all) of the rights conferred upon men, and are widely viewed as citizens. This has not, however, spelled the end of phallic masculinity. Instead, the phallic mode has broadened in modernity, especially in the USA, into a formation I will refer to as phallic agency. The phallic agent, whether male, female, or something else, is imagined to possess the invulnerability and activity characteristic of phallic masculinity. In the discourse of phallic agency, agency is equated with initiative as opposed to receptivity or transmission, with invulnerability as opposed to 'being a victim'. Agency becomes an either/or proposition: either I am fully self-initiating, acting from my own deepest motives and beliefs (that, of course, are uniquely mine and not the result of socialisation or other inscriptions), letting nothing stand between me and my dreams, or I am a victim, a weakling, a dupe, a slave. To the phallic agent, there are actors and there are the acted-upon. Although, traditionally, this division was held to map neatly onto men and women, white and non-white, the discourse of equality over the past three centuries has fostered lines of migration among these. Without changing the binary, those previously held to be passive have found ways to imagine themselves as phallic and have made claims to equality based on their shared phallic status. This, of course, is not all that has happened; social movements have also challenged the binary between phallic agents and victims, often quite powerfully. Movements of oppressed peoples always embody the tension between claiming political attention on the basis of what has been done to one and acting on one's own behalf; such movements are movements of victim/agents. Nonetheless, in American culture these binaries remain defaults for understanding social status, and the position of the victim/agent is continually refused and vilified. The stereotype of 'victim feminism', propounded by popular authors male and female alike, concedes that women may and should be able to be independent, equal citizens while excoriating virtually all feminist analyses for their 'obsession' with barriers to equality and independence (Deutchman, 1998). The phallic response is to deny that women or other groups are systematically disempowered, and to view as insulting the claim that they are.

Investment in the phallic imaginary anatomy enables us to understand not only the overt rejection of those whose bodies do not conform to that imaginary anatomy, but also the stigmatisation of civil rights claims. There are at least two discourses on civil rights in the USA, and their contradictory reception and employment are understandable through the lens of the phallic body politic. These discourses are linked to differing understandings about what is being claimed and who is claiming it.

The first discourse, familiar since before the American Revolution, demands certain basic rights for citizens, understood to be normatively masculine. These rights include safety within and control over one's household; protection from violence, both by individuals and the state; and the right to participate in public decision-making through freedom of speech and association. Insisting upon these rights is part of being a man in the USA; failure to do so would be 'wimpy', ignoble, and a demonstration of weakness. Masculinity in the USA is closely bound up with the maintenance of one's rights.

When others use this discourse, however, their discordant personal features threaten the body politic. What in the hands of white heterosexual men serves as the foundation of liberty becomes an attack on society when extended to those who were previously either incorporated into the polity through the 'head' of the household or excluded from recognition. The Revolutionary generation and those that followed confronted the dilemma of how to claim the language of equality and natural law for themselves while denying it to others; this task was usually managed, to the extent that it was managed, first, by claiming irrevocable differences between the characters and capacities of male citizens and those they sought to exclude, and, second, by the division between public and private realms. Public equality of men relied upon their mutual privilege and domination of women, children, and people of colour (Pateman, 1988; Kerber, 1997). With the rise of feminism and consequent refigurings of law, the demand for safety within one's household becomes a ban on marital assault, rape, and incest. The recognition that many citizens live within a household, and that they may not in fact share the interest of the eldest male, allows the state to penetrate the household in new ways, piercing the castle walls and besieging that 'miniature fatherland' through which Rousseau believed that attachment to the larger fatherland, the state, was accomplished (Rousseau, 1911, p.326). In Rousseau's time, as in ours, 'the desire to retain in the traditional form of marriage some safeguard of order against the destructive tendencies of modern individualism, cut across the familiar divides between conservative and liberal, left and right' (Vogel, 1991, p.76). It also cuts across lines of gender and race. Civil liberties meant to foster the independence of male citizens against the state become instruments of destruction when wielded by those who cannot legitimately claim to be 'heads'.

The shift in the nature of rights depending upon who has them is only part of the story, however. Just as important is the change in understandings of what rights are needed for basic citizenship. The second discourse of rights addresses what T. H. Marshall calls 'social rights', that is, rights to education, decent housing, and food (Marshall, 1992). These rights have never been completely accepted in the USA. Although they are widely acknowledged as prerequisites for the independence associated with citizenship, the individualism of the USA has blocked their full incorporation into rights. This failure is not simply due to an abstraction that we may call individualism, however. Rather, the particular form of American individualism is crucial for understanding the resistance to these social rights. American individualism, like its republican counterpart, is deeply gendered. In fact, it is not too much to say that 'the classic statements of American individualism are best understood as guides to masculine identity' (Kerber, 1997, p.202). From Emerson to Horatio Alger to contemporary fiction and political writing, the heroic individual is male and masculine. He works hard, he thinks for himself, and he stands firm for his principles and his family in the face of danger and seduction.

The political experience of groups figured as non-phallic makes clear that civil rights are not a single package with a consistent response, either within individuals or within communities. The demand for civil rights puts one in the position of admitting one's vulnerability and dependence on the larger society. Such admissions are often viewed as whining excuses by those who want to imagine themselves as intact and their society as composed of similarly bounded individuals. Phallic agents of whatever group see the admission of inequality as the abandonment of agency, and so are just as prone to attack those speaking in their behalf as they are to question those who would exclude them. The American citizen is figured in popular imagination as an effective agent, capable of making real change. That figure both endorses and works against movements for equality. On the one hand, for the citizen to make change she must see problems and convince others of their gravity and the possibility of change. On the other, admitting some problems threatens the citizen's certainty that she is in fact a citizen, opening the door to feelings of rejection and abandonment that she may not be willing to confront. In order to become an oppositional agent, one must first admit one's discontent and present ineffectiveness; in a culture in which feelings of inefficacy are held to be pathological, individuals are reluctant to follow that path. This continuing dynamic of social movements must be confronted, and not simply diagnosed as false consciousness; without finding ways of penetrating phallic masculinity, movements for change will continually face the charge that they, rather than the circumstances they oppose, stand in the way of equality.

The Body Under Siege

Republican political theorists such as Machiavelli and Rousseau have agreed that liberty is the fruit of struggle, and that its maintenance requires constant vigilance and valour. But if struggle must be continual, against whom is it to be directed? One of the greatest dangers of civic republicanism is its need for an enemy, whether internal or external, in order to marshal the citizen body. This marshalling is simultaneously a constitution, both of the enemy and of the citizen self. The perception of threat is not incidental to or subsequent to the construction of the republican citizen self, but is integral to that constitution. The citizen must constantly ward off threats to the autonomy and sovereignty of the body/polity in order to establish his own autonomy and sovereignty. Citizenship is about virility, that is, active defence of that which is threatened, rather than being the victim of threat. At moments of threat, republican rhetoric denies the threat to masculine individuals and, instead, figures the country as threatened, needing the defence of her sons and the obedience of her daughters. Thus, anxiety about personal security is disavowed and displaced onto another vulnerable body.

The trope of the body politic works powerfully to transform contests within society into attacks on society. Stigmatised groups may become threats to 'the public health' and the 'moral fibre of the nation', imagined agents of disintegration. These threats are threats to the phallic status of the public body: the body politic is threatened by 'becoming soft', by being 'susceptible', 'docile', 'passive', or 'infected', in short, by being either penetrated or vulnerable to penetration.

In the USA, sexuality has been a primary site for fears of contamination of the body politic. It is possible to understand this in liberal terms, as simply the result of ignorance or outmoded religious strictures, and that is not a false understanding. It is, however, incomplete. These fears are integral to the phallic self, and mitigating them requires a transformation of that self. The challenge of queers is not simply about sexual difference, but is about the very passions that constitute American understandings of citizenship.

The threat to the phallic body of the citizen posed by homosexuality is by now clear to many observers. The fears about gays in the military, fears that cluster around the shower and the barracks, are so clear as to need no analysis. Heterosexual soldiers' repeated expressions of concern that someone might be looking at them or wanting to touch them, expressions solicited and encouraged by their military superiors and by senators, make manifest a host of assumptions about masculine sexuality and the privilege of looking. For these men, being a man means being the initiator, the gazer, the penetrator, but never the one penetrated by gaze or by body, never the object of another's initiative. Homosexuality here becomes problematic because, as Bordo notes, it 'both embraces and violates masculinity'; while homosexuality is the most explicit celebration of male bodies and masculinity, it also is a threat to the system of sexual difference within which masculinity takes on meaning. Fear of violation and its activating assumptions are present not only in discussions of the military, but in virtually every treatment of queers in politics. Whether the individual body or the national body, some body is being threatened by strange desire.

The entry of acknowledged homosexuality into this scene is a threat for several reasons. First, acknowledgement of some men's erotic love threatens the structure of denial on which fraternity depends. Following Freud, Judith Butler argues that 'social feeling and citizenship' are founded on a desexualised and externalised homosexuality (Butler, 1997, p.120). In the place of desire, we find social bonds as well as resentments. In this argument, the acknowledgement of civic or fraternal love is fraught with disruptive potential, and seems to mandate the withdrawal of civic passion altogether. By making homosociality no longer innocent, gay men threaten not only the phallic masculine self, but the possibilities for love among heterosexual men. This is, of course, a great loss to republican men, one they might rightly resent. The homosexual man becomes the spoiler, the wet blanket at the fraternal slumber party.

Acknowledging queer love would also endanger the polity through the reintroduction of particular love. If love between men is possible, it threatens the polity just as romantic love for women did. Love between men, however, cannot be dealt with by isolating the potential object of affection and contest; since such love may ignite from any man who opens himself to it, the opening itself must be squashed. This can be ensured (never successfully) only by seeking out and removing those who manifest the possibility of opening to other men. As the history of many armies shows us, this fear is not an inevitable feature of republican regimes. It may, however, be inevitable for modern regimes, with their particular configurations of masculinity, fraternity, and independence.

Republicanism has never been a congenial discourse for women, who have been figured as the private property of men, as virtuous mothers, or as threats to male solidarity, but never as citizens in their own right. The position of lesbians, then, cannot be neatly appended to the fear of male homosexuality. Following the heterologic of sexual difference, lesbians might be expected to be more perfectly phallic than gay men, and thus carrying more potential to be model citizens. This has not been the case. Instead, concerns about lesbianism appear in public in the USA via larger fears about feminism and women's equality or power, or women's potential to corrupt children. Although lesbians in the military are discharged at a much higher rate than are men, they have not been an important part of the public discussion about the military because the military remains an institution saturated with masculinity. To discern lesbian citizens, we need to look in another site of public debate, marriage and family.

Mainstream lesbian and gay activists have stressed the fact that we have families and often have children. The implication is that we are 'normal', with the same cares and hopes as heterosexual families. This has been a much more prominent arena for lesbians, in the public imagination if not in fact, than the military. By appealing to the image of the mother and the father, activists desexualise queers. Arguments for marriage suggest that marriage would end promiscuity and promote stability among queers, thus making them less threatening to the dominant society. This argument smacks of republican understandings of the home as the fount of virtue and an intimacy that is inappropriate for liberal political institutions, but nonetheless crucial in the formation of liberal character.

This argument has several flaws. First, as many others have pointed out, such arguments appeal to heterosexuals by colluding with them against queers who value alternatives to the nuclear family. They drive a wedge between 'respectable' gays and lesbians and 'freaks', thus failing to address the underlying fears that the line between the two is unreliable. By trying to insinuate themselves into the body politic, they do not challenge the ways that modern American political discourse understands threats to the body politic. By arguing that most queers are no different from their heterosexual neighbours, they do not open the polity to a greater appreciation of difference. Of course, many have argued that simply gaining admission is an opening for difference, because queer families are not like heterosexual ones; however, recent research on lesbian mothers and gay and lesbian families suggests that they are often not very different, and fail to challenge larger social understandings about gender, privacy, and parenting (Lewin, 1993). In this situation, the admission of some does not challenge current boundaries of the body politic, but may, in fact, reinforce them. In the quest to be accepted, those making these arguments often fail to appreciate the ways in which standards of 'normal' marriage make outlaws out of alternative forms.

Rather than opening the category of marriage to loosening, the visibility of alternatives is just as likely to generate fears of chaos in the home. When features seen as outside of or opposed to domesticity, such as 'lawless' sexuality, enter the home, the result is more likely to be fierce reaction and protection of the body under siege. This does not mean that such entrances and combinations should not be engaged in, but that the consequences must be taken seriously, rather than dismissed in a celebration of carnivalesque dislocations. As communities are constructed around certain conceptions of appropriate bodily attributes and comportment, challenges to those conceptions amount to subversion of the community.

To make this point, I would like to examine a somewhat different debate about marriage. Just about a century ago, Congress was faced with a series of decisions about polygamy. The practice of polygamy among Mormons, most notably in Utah but also in Idaho, was the subject of popular outcry as these territories moved toward statehood. Groups opposed to statehood demanded laws banning polygamy throughout the USA, and prospective voters in Utah were forced to sign an oath forswearing 'polygamy, bigamy, unlawful cohabitation, incest, adultery, and fornication' (US Congress, 1890, p.1). Such oaths did not settle the issue; legislators and citizens continued to hunt down polygamists and to ban them from citizenship rights. Mormons were characterised as 'absolutely treacherous', suffering from moral decay, whose children were 'a menace to the future of our country' (US Congress, 1902, p.2) because of the 'licentiousness' to which they were exposed. The full rhetoric of the body under siege was mobilised against the heathens, who had 'no right to be called American citizens' (US Congress, 1902, p.13). Polygamy was a 'disease' being 'scattered' around the country and, just as 'evil is catching in a way that goodness never is' (US Congress, 1902, p.8), if not stopped it would soon drive out decent family values. No compromise was acceptable, nothing short of national action would suffice: when the body is under siege, compromise or rapprochement cannot be afforded. What is a compromise between a body and an invading agent?

The Mormons, many of whom now spearhead the drive against same-sex marriage, felt that they valued marriage as much as anyone in the USA. One might imagine them currently arguing for polygamy as an alternative family form, had not the desire for statehood forced a change in Church policy a century ago. What they saw as true, holy marriage was not seen as an 'alternative understanding' or an 'expansion' of marriage by their antagonists, but as a dagger pointed at the heart of marriage and family life, and through that to the whole body politic. That is what opponents of same-sex marriage see today – not an opportunity to domesticate those promiscuous queers, but the introduction of chaos into the core of society. Rather than making queers safe for the world, same-sex marriage would make marriage incoherent. It would erase the line between licence and order by importing licence into the heart of the ordered family. This is why Congress passed, and President Clinton signed, a Defense of Marriage Act. Those who see marriage as a vehicle for domestication and normalisation found this a bizarre rhetorical move, but I think it makes sense if we read it as queers changing marriage. Such a change, like allowing polygamy, amounts to nullifying the meaning and sanctity of marriage.

Lesbians emerge in this scenario as the bad mother. Like the polygamous mother, lesbians induct their children into sin in such a way that their children do not even recognise it as sin. Appeals to maternal love and examples of happy families will continually confront the fear that their love will lead their children to accept that which should not be accepted. Maternal love then becomes not domesticating and instructive, but seductive.

Does this mean that change is impossible? Of course not. Conceptual and value systems change over time, though they also show remarkable stability. It means that we cannot rely on tactics that would seem to make queers 'safe for society', because the encounter between societies and those they see as outsiders is never resolved simply by bringing the outsiders in. Very often outsiders are outside for a reason that goes to the heart of the structure of that society. Denying that fact may be part of a struggle to redefine the dominant understandings of that society, but it may also fail to offer more than palliatives.

Citizenship for those whose bodies and passions do not conform to phallic modes will require not simply citizenship for queers, but a thorough queering of citizenship itself. Such a queering must include a challenge to the ideology of independence and masculinity. As the grounds for citizenship, the ideology of independence and its not-so-covert gendered association continue to make strangers out of women, queers, and others who do not fit the ideal of the autonomous individual. 'The community' remains the community of male heads of households, with their families in a zone somewhere between public and private. Activism that challenges associations between heterosexuality, whiteness, and masculinity with autonomous rationality will inevitably confront the rhetoric of the citizen body and the body politic, and my earlier remarks should not be construed as suggesting that reaction is a reason not to engage in such challenges. We must, however, seek to understand fully the contours and the functioning of such rhetoric. We cannot simply use liberal arguments and trust in the triumph of reason, both because history shows us that reason does not always triumph and because reason itself is bound up in the contention. Disentangling the elements of citizenship rhetoric may enable us to perform micro-challenges, placing pressure on weak points and easing republican discourse into forms that are less rigid and oppositional. This, at any rate, is my hope.

REFERENCES

Berlant, L. 1997. *The Queen of American Goes to Washington City: Essays on Sex and Citizenship*. Durham, Duke University Press.

Bordo, S. 1993. *Unbearable Weight: Feminism, Western Culture, and the Body*. Berkeley, University of California Press.

1997. Reading the male body. In *Building Bodies*, ed. P. Moore. New Brunswick (NJ), Rutgers University Press.

Butler, J. 1990. *Gender Trouble: Feminism and the Subversion of Identity*. New York, Routledge.

Connell, R. W. 1995. *Masculinities*. Berkeley, University of California Press.

Deutchman, I. E. 1998. It's (not) just the victim in me: gender and power in the 1990s. *Women and Politics*, 19/1, pp.1–18.

Easthope, A. 1990. *What a Man's Gotta Do: Masculinity in Popular Culture*. London, Palatin.

Fraser, N. and Gordon, L. 1994. A genealogy of dependency: tracing a keyword of the U.S. welfare state. *Signs: Journal of Women in Culture and Society*, 19, pp.1–29.

Galston, W. 1991. *Liberal Purposes*. Cambridge, Cambridge University Press.

Gatens, M. 1991. Corporeal representation in/and the body politic. In *Cartographies: Poststructuralism and the Mapping of Bodies and Spaces*, eds. R. Diprose and R. Ferrell. Sydney, Allen and Unwin.

Grosz, E. 1994. *Volatile Bodies: Toward a Corporeal Feminism*. Bloomington, Indiana University Press.

Halperin, D. 1990. *One Hundred Years of Homosexuality*. New York, Routledge.

Hartsock, N. 1983. *Money, Sex, and Power*. Boston, Northeastern University Press.

Irigary, Luce. 1985. *Speculum of the Other Woman*. Trans. Gillian C. Gill. Ithaca (N.Y.), Cornell University Press.

Kerber, L. 1997. *Toward an Intellectual History of Women*. Chapel Hill, University of North Carolina Press.

Lewin, E. 1993. *Lesbian Mothers: Accounts of Gender in American Culture*. Ithaca (NY), Cornell University Press.

Lincoln, A. 1992. *Selected Writings*. ed. and intro. H. Mitgang. New York, Bantam.

Marshall, T. M. 1992. Citizenship and social class. In *Citizenship and Social Class*, eds. T. M. Marshall and T. Bottomore. London, Pluto.

Monoson, S. 1994. Citizen as *erastes*: erotic imagery and the idea of reciprocity in the Periclean funeral oration. *Political Theory*, 22/2, pp.253–76.

O'Neill, J. 1985. *Five Bodies*. Ithaca, Cornell University Press.

Pateman, C. 1988. *The Sexual Contract*. Palo Alto (CA), Stanford University Press.

1989. *The Disorder of Women: Democracy, Feminism, and Political Theory*. Palo Alto (CA), Stanford University Press.

Pitkin, H. F. 1984. *Fortune is a Woman: Gender and Politics in the Thought of Niccolo Machiavelli*. Berkeley, University of California Press.

Pocock, J. G. A. 1975. *The Machiavellian Moment: Florentine Political Thought and the Atlantic Republican Tradition*. Princeton, Princeton University Press.

Roosevelt, T. 1958. *The Free Citizen*.

Rousseau, J-J. 1911. *Emile*. Trans. B. Foxley. New York, E. P. Dutton.

Schatzki, T. R. and Natter, W. eds. 1996. *The Social and Political Body*. New York, Guilford.

Shklar, J. 1991. *American Citizenship: The Quest for Inclusion*. Cambridge (MA), Harvard University Press.

US Congress. House of Representatives. 1890. *Amendment to Section 5352, Revised Statutes*. 51st Cong., 1st sess, Report 1811.

1902. *Polygamy*. Committee on the Judiciary. 57th Cong., 1st sess.

Vogel, Ursula. 1991. Is citizenship gender-specific? In *The Frontiers of Citizenship*, ed. Ursula Vogel and Michael Moran. New York, St. Martin's.

Waldby, C. 1996. *AIDS and the Body Politic: Biomedicine and Sexual Difference*. London, Routledge.

Young, I. M. 1997. *Intersecting Voices: Dilemmas of Gender, Political Philosophy, and Public Policy*. Princeton, Princeton University Press.

4

Is the Postmodern Self a Feminised Citizen?

ELOISE A. BUKER

I am raising a question about the politics of the postmodern self by asking if postmodernism has developed an understanding of the self by feminising generic man? The modern American self is an autonomous, integrated, rational self-made human who claims to be at one with the universe, seeks an integrated sovereign centre, and experiences freedom as the lack of interference from other persons, governments, or social institutions. The self is free from commitments that limit expression and the maximisation of pleasures. Michael Sandel has named this modern version of the self, 'the unencumbered self' (1996, pp.111–19). This self has continuity over time in that a single unique body contains it, and the body's skin serves to mark the boundary between the self and other beings. Accomplishments are measured in terms of material monuments that live on beyond the body's life: books, buildings, art works, and corporations. 'Eternal' life is gained through their production. Supported by secular humanism, this self has become not only independent of other humans, but also separate from both cosmological and natural forces, both of which become either the objects of control or subjects of negotiation. The study of this being's centre is psychology, which has become modernity's most popularised science because of its ability to penetrate, explain, and even modify the inner self (Levine, 1992). Despite the lack of sex organs, this inner being is symbolised as either masculine or feminine. Sigmund Freud, Karl Jung, and their followers describe the moral development of this inner self in sexualised imagery that features self-control and constraint.

While pre-moderns told a tale of individuals who depended on 'their' God and King, the secular democratic modern tale places even greater emphasis on individual independence and relies even more on reason as a constraining force. Displacing both cosmological and scientific narratives, the modern state has emerged as a centre for moral constraints. Explaining that humans are self-centred beings who use society to satisfy their own pleasures, utilitarians have difficulty accounting for affection. What has made sense of this separated self is another sort of self — a complementary being who depends on others, who relies on feelings rather than reason, and who experiences freedom as collective action with other persons, governments, and social institutions. This self is a self-sacrificing, privatised female whose main passion is taking care of others. As the late twentieth century increased the secularisation of public life, women became even more important figures for preserving altruistic values and un-reasonable impulses of goodwill toward others. Men's autonomy is crystallised in the context of women's dependency. Privatised selves are represented by feminine images of 'soft' boundaries with altruistic urges. The boundary of the feminine private self is not clear. Even biology fails *her* because during pregnancy her outer skin no longer serves as a clear boundary between herself and another. Her body raises such questions as: where should her control over her body end and that of society begin? When is 'she' one body, and when is she two? American society imagines women as connected selves whose inner spirit seeks to connect with external forces and to aid others in doing the same. A woman is the shadow image of the autonomous self.

This independent modern self is in tension with the community, which symbolises connections among persons. Politically, this tension plays a key role in the distinction between liberals, who emphasise the importance of civil rights that protect citizens from social interventions, and communitarians, who are more concerned about the responsibilities that citizens have to and for one another. Calling the communitarian self the 'obligated self', Diane Margolis draws from Charles Taylor to argue that community bonds depend on obligations formed by family, generational connections, and affection (Margolis, 1998). One strategy for resolving this tension between the individual and the community is to create areas of specialisation for each of these two sorts of selves: the autonomous self and the relational self. The former is intended for political-economic life, and the latter for home and friendship. Thus, women do connections; men do independence. This gender specialisation means that these two modern Western selves require each other to function as complete human beings because each one represents really only a half-self. Since the autonomous self cannot acknowledge the need for another, that self has to be presented as the one in charge, and the relational self can serve as the dependent subordinate one, who nurtures others. This hierarchy is played out in a sex/gender system. As men play the autonomous self and women the dependent self, American society attempts to symbolise a complete individual through a compulsive heterosexuality that fuses the two selves to create a whole human. This sense of incompleteness may help explain why US novels, popular songs, and visual arts present the heterosexual romance as a primary icon.

While the golden mean between the autonomous and communitarian self might produce a fully human self who is capable of both autonomy and community, this mean cannot be achieved without crossing the sex barrier because the two functions have been gendered. Even communitarians who favour community and connections have trouble drawing females into their self-understandings. Eileen Bresnahan shows how communitarians privilege male citizenship (1994). Although there has been some movement toward androgyny, the autonomous self is so masculinised that even androgyny threatens male identity. Thus, moderns have inherited a complementary social scheme that requires the heterosexual family to make it work. While the state needs both types of persons, it has privileged the autonomous masculinised self. Thus, men represent women (males constitute 90 per cent of the Congress), and citizenship is masculinised (Hartsock, 1983). Zillah Eisenstein demonstrates in *The Female Body and the Law* that the male body is an underlying assumption in American legal discourse (1988). While feminism has made some headway in challenging the male as the representative of humanity, the autonomous masculine self still has represented the modern ideal, and liberal feminists work to demonstrate that women can also be autonomous independent selves.

The autonomous masculinised self is politically important in how it defines responsibility and constructs the boundaries between persons. First, autonomy locates responsibility in the individual as opposed to the community. 'He' is considered the site of sovereignty; the new king reigns, and 'his' home is his castle. Individual responsibility plays a central role in public life because the individual represents the smallest and most basic unit of the polity. Responsibility is seldom accorded to body parts; for example, his arm did it. Nor is responsibility often assigned to the community-at-large, that is, everyone did it. When a state or community errs or succeeds, some individual is blamed or credited, whether that be Hitler, Lincoln, Clinton, or Elvis Presley. When a government is in trouble, citizens look to place a new individual at the top. The assumption is that the individual is rational and integrated. The irrational (mentally ill) and split, unintegrated person is less competent and so less responsible because independence implies a singular, unified self in which the mind controls the body. Yet, social life depends on flexible emotional citizens whose minds respond to their bodies. Again, the modern solution is a gendered division of labour in which women specialise in flexibility, responsiveness, and feelings.

Autonomy asserts the importance of maintaining boundaries between individuals. The body represents this boundary, often represented by the phrase 'that my freedom ends when my fist hits his face'.[1] For example, habeas corpus asserts that the person has a right to their own body and that that right supersedes state claims. But the pregnant female body confuses this boundary between the body and the state. Resorting to autonomy as a measure for personhood, the state has privileged the foetus, who can survive on its 'own' outside the womb. The female body suggests an organic link among persons from their conception to their death. Bodies do not just touch; they commingle. Modern females both experience and represent the postmodern image of 'leaky' borders in which boundaries are less than clear cut.

I will argue that the postmodern self is very similar to this complementary feminine self. My argument is not that the postmodern self employs Carol Gilligan's story of two types of persons: predominately males who use principled and individualised understandings of the world and predominately females who employ relational concepts to understand the world (Gilligan, 1982). Nor is my tale about a feminist victory that has achieved a power reversal with women on top and men on the bottom. Rather, my tale examines how the postmodern self echoes characteristics of the old modern female. The modern story about women as dependent persons, whose virtues are responsiveness and flexibility, represents 'her' relationship to others with an ethics that emphasises care and context over self-interest and independence (Gilligan, 1982; Tronto, 1993). Like the postmodern self, she sees herself made and remade by cultural practices that constitute her (Shapiro, 1981, 1992). In contrast to her male counterpart, her performances appear less unified and more fragmentary, as she plays wife, mother, sister, friend, politician, counsellor, worker, and so on. Her body manifests the intersection of human life in both a material and symbolic sense.

My story asks: is this postmodern self a version of the modern female? If so, can it escape the second-class citizenship that still shadows American females? To explore this, I am asking three questions. First, can a fragmented, culturally diverse self that displaces the unitary, autonomous self be a responsible citizen? Or must the postmodern view give up agency and follow the tradition of the early modern female? Second, can a political ethic emerge from culturally dependent citizens? Or is the postmodern self locked into a web of relationships that makes it unable to access an ethical code? Third, can words and materiality mix so that borders are contingent, fuzzy, and leaky rather than clear cut? Can politics include the examination of symbols without reducing the world to a text?

Fragmenting the Individual Citizen: Beyond Masculinity

The story of the modern US self begins in pre-modern times with the Greek notion of a balanced, ordered human composed by reason, spirit, and appetite. This self image is fortified by Christian narratives that assert the uniqueness of persons, united under a God-ordered moral universe. These images, along with others, have produced a modern secular understanding of the self that cherishes autonomy, reason, and unity. This autonomous being is understood as the primary unit of social organisation, just as the atom is the primary unit of the physical world. Just as the atom holds a substance together, the individual makes societies work. Hoyt L. Edge describes how the metaphor of the atom permeates modern understandings of humanity and constructs freedom as a lack of constraint (1994). Nature directs 'us'. This view of the self emphasises individual desires over community desires, which may threaten constraints. Diane Rothbard Margolis calls this understanding of the self 'The Exchanger' and explains how modern American culture, relying on this view of the self, understands public life as a marketplace for property exchange (1998, pp.15–40). This fits well with utilitarian social values in which the self serves as the primary centre for commitment and moral authority. So divorce, broken friendships, ruptured romances, and contingent communities are to be expected. The idealised person is self-made, self-centred, and self-sufficient.

In this story, power is manifested by controlling 'external' forces, especially other humans and nature. However, even as a John Wayne was emerging as the American archetype, 'he' experienced difficulties. Although the old cowboy/sheriff figure has made an appearance in the American Presidency, his style is outdated. Having tamed as well as maimed the West, he has come to realise that he just cannot do 'it' all by himself. Even the modern cop who has replaced him as the law-and-order figure is partnered. American television has replaced Serpico with partnered figures found in *Law and Order*, *Cagney and Lacy*, and *Sweet Justice*. Matlock has a female colleague, and Jessica, the mystery queen, relies upon Doc to help her solve the puzzle. The lone ranger gives way to co-operative egalitarian male-female teams. The late-modern hero/heroine works with others, emphasises collaborative management styles, depends on technological power, and employs democratic decision-making not only in politics, but also at work and in the home. Although he or she continues to exercise some independence, each works within a social system, a town, and a bureaucracy. And, fixing the system is the responsibility of the team, not that of a singular figure.

In place of the lone figure, dedicated to transforming entire towns, nations, or corporations, the contemporary figure(s), whether male or female, take on less grandiose goals with a more playful and lighter style (Kundera, 1984; Kariel, 1989). Even the evening news anchors have become more frivolous as they banter among themselves. We Americans take '*our*selves' less seriously. Setting aside the dreams of a revolution, citizens find reformations more possible. The postmodern self, like William Shakespeare's Puck, is not clearly male or female, and he/she delights in confusions, reversals, and disruptions. He/she teases the system instead of rebelling against it. American figures that come readily to mind include Jay Leno, Madonna, Newt Gingrich (who sometimes appears more willing to disrupt than to rule), Rosanne Barr, Lily Tomlin, Michael Jackson, and perhaps the slimmer version of Oprah Winfrey.

Like the old feminine self, who was supposed to use her wiles to move her fellow citizens toward change, so the postmodern 'Puck' hopes to induce change by personal wit, witticisms, and seductive rhetoric, and he/she is more likely to rely on charm than political revolt, war, and economic sanctions. But this charm has a bite to it, an irony, that still hopes for political transformations (Ferguson, 1993; Rorty, 1989), even though revolution seems to be the impossible dream of the bygone macho citizen, who merely fooled himself into thinking he could make 'such' a difference, or even that such a difference was desirable. Embodying flexible fragmentary selves, postmodern Pucks change as they change others. The pregnant woman might serve as a better image of the citizen than the lone warrior (Ruddick, 1989). The inner/outer centre does not hold, nor is it supposed to. The new postmodern self decentres old versions of autonomy by explaining that 'the' inner self is composed by cultural constructs that even shape what counts as 'inner'. An ordered, reasonable society and an orderly person are cultural images, not manifestations of harmonious universal codes.

Even individual experience is explained by postmoderns as the reflection of cultural training and, thus, cannot serve as a source of truth. Experiences are not raw, untouched phenomena, but culturally mediated events. For example, we Americans fall in love because our culture talks about falling in love. Experience is not the stuff of which selves are made, but cultural patterns that citizens receive. Given a different cultural heritage, the experience would differ. For many feminists, discrediting experience is particularly problematic because it has served as a check against patriarchy (Bell and Klein, 1996), but the postmodern view of experience also echoes feminist arguments. By claiming that experience is the result of cultural beliefs rather than sources of truth, postmoderns cast the validity of men's experiences into doubt, suggesting that all experiences are merely replays of cultural practices and ideologies.

For those interested in public life, the critique of this inner core presents a problem because modernity linked responsibility with rationality, autonomy, and unity. The autonomous, inner self was responsible for intention and motivation. In contrast, the postmodern story explains that the self lacks such an autonomous inner core and instead makes decisions in the context of a finite variety of possibilities presented in a particular cultural context. However, this position does not liberate citizens from responsibility, for cultural patterns do not determine choices, but only provide parameters for them. As Susan Hekman points out, postmodernism does not turn individuals into cultural dupes (1990). Within cultural contexts, there are choices to be made, even though those choices are not infinite.

But if humans have no unique inner core, how are creativity and innovation possible? The story about cultural change might go something like this. The self, while given its basic structure by the culture, has choices to make. It selects aspects of the culture that are mixed and matched to compose a self. The composition of this self is not unitary and fixed but is put together for moments and events. Nevertheless, it is sufficiently together to be enacted as a single life. This story of selfhood decentres the autonomous inner being, a central feature of the modern self, without giving up individual choice. But the choices are the result of activities and performances; it is not that activities are the result of the choices made by an inner, untouched source (Butler, 1990). For example, the old Hebraic-Christian story of woman was that she was made from man, and the more current television version is that she is shaped by the man 'in her life'. Thus, the story of a self who is culturally made is similar to the old tale of the modern woman, who was not seen as self-made but instead as culturally composed. The oft-told tale of *Pygmalion*, *My Fair Lady*, or even 'Cinderella' embodies the modern tale of woman's climb from rags to riches through the acquisition of cultural experiences. In this respect, the postmodern self and the old modern feminine self are both dependent persons made by others, in contrast to modern man, who makes himself all by himself.

But contradictory demands have made it hard for the modern female to integrate family, career, and social-civic responsibilities. Getting her act together seems impossible. Her duties fragment her life by pulling her in many directions. Jane Flax shows how postmodern thought explains that such fragmentation is not a flaw but, instead, is natural and ordinary, even desirable (1990). The postmodern self, rather than deploring inconsistencies and contradictions, accepts them and makes them part of the self. This acceptance displaces the old questions about the boundary between the self and others and raises a new question. Which set of selves (which cultures and communities) will be used to develop a self? In other words, which cultures and communities will be foregrounded to form a self? In the US context, this question emerges as the struggle between state and federal authority. Obligations that arise out of loyalties to states, cities, regions, religions, ethnicities, classes, genders, sexualities, professions, philosophies, and others complicate citizen identities. A postmodern conception of the self makes sense out of this confusing matrix of demands because it does not attempt to fit them all into a single hierarchy, but instead constructs a narrative about life that shifts among them. The old political question, 'Who am I?' dissolves into a new postmodern political question, 'Which political communities do I join, and which ones do I refuse to quit?'

At the level of aesthetics, the postmodern self replaces the romantic artist as the lone creator with a more social view of an artist who creates in concert with others. Robert Browning's *Fra Lippo Lippi* gives way to Judy Chicago's *The Dinner Party*, which was composed by a large team of artists. Is it possible to tell a tale about creativity because it does not require an autonomous single hero to author the tale? Can a collective story be enacted by a cast of characters, many of whom play multiple parts? Is artistic production necessarily the result of the sole actions of an isolated romantic figure? Can rugged individualism give way to fuzzy boundaries and coalitions of contingent selves or communities? Certainly, Butler argues for coalitions, and Richard Rorty explains that selves are contingent beings (Butler, 1990; Rorty, 1989). On the other hand, Nancy Hartsock objects to these formulations because the decentred subject comes at the time when women are just beginning to be considered subjects (1990, pp.157–75). My argument is that the fragmented subject decentres men by drawing on the modern female self and thereby creates gender equity.

The modern Euro-American middle-class heterosexual female already had to acquire a fragmented identity to function as a citizen. She was expected to be independent in public and dependent and subordinate in private. Attempts to make this work involve splitting her into two persons – a public and a private person. So, the fragmentary self better fits the modern woman's conflicting identities as citizen, worker, and nurturer. Since black women have had a longer work history and so have avoided some images of femininity as incompetence, they have found themselves somewhat less torn by the work/home poles. Nevertheless, African-American women have experienced identity conflicts as they resist social norms that ask them to choose between their identities as 'women' and as blacks (Hooks, 1995; Collins, 1991). Lesbians, whose identities sometimes become truncated by the limited performances of a masculine-butch and a feminine-femme, encounter other versions of these contradictions. Lesbian theory illuminates how heterosexism has made integrating private and public life difficult (Sedgwick, 1990; Fuss, 1991, 1989). Requiring citizens to be unified and singular creates value conflicts and leads to unsatisfactory compartmentalisations. While the old, even pre-modern, ideology treasured a unified self, modernity made the existence of such a self impossible.

This impossibility has made the postmodern fragmentary self especially attractive. Obviously, it is immediately attractive to women because it makes a virtue out of what has been a problem – the fragmentary character of women's lives. Women can seek to meet the challenges of fragmentation rather than work to overcome it. As men identify with women, they, too, may find this fragmentary image comforting. Released from the requirement that one be all-together, the fragmented self can play contradictory roles. No longer are citizens stuck with a singular identity (black, female, or middle class), but can be many things at once (black-white-Chicana, bisexual, middle class, and masculine-feminine).

According to Judith Butler, such identities are formed by actions; they do not emerge from some central essential individual characteristics (1990). Hawaii's multiethnic composition provides an example of how this operates. In one context, a Chinese-Filipino-Irish woman might emphasise her Chinese grandmother, in another, her Filipino grandfather, and in a third, her Irish-American mother. For Butler, the self is composed by acting in political situations (1990). I am suggesting that everyday social acts compose and recompose persons as they enact cultural traditions such as cooking rice, telling stories, and staging demonstrations. The postmodern self cherishes mixing cultures and supports continual change in place of philosophical or ideological consistency. Gender-bending and ethnic-switching are not disloyal to the self's core or its origins.[2]

This articulation of the multiplicity of selves that form individuals avoids identity politics. Finding pure blacks, true Anglo-Saxons, or the 'real' feminist woman is abandoned in favour of finding persons who can commit to a set of limited political goals. This fragmentation undercuts the puritanical qualities assigned to such characteristics as race/ethnicity, sex, and sexuality. While this postmodern self does not anticipate a pure revolution, she/he anticipates the benefits and drawbacks of particular actions. Displacing the old John Wayne, the postmodern Puck draws from a host of selves to create social change.

Connecting Selves: Beyond Humanism

G. W. F. Hegel's notion of the state, as well as Simone de Beauvoir's interpretation of woman as the permanent other, show the political dimensions in forming interpretations of the self (Hegel, 1977; Beauvoir, 1952). Drawing on philosophical hermeneutics, Paul Ricoeur explains that the self becomes meaningful in the context of an other (1992, p.297). Using the concept of self-interpretation, developed by Hans-Georg Gadamer and Husserl, Ricoeur argues that a fully developed self depends on the ability of a person to see themselves as an 'other'. Ricoeur explains that the 'hermeneutics of the self' develops by dialogical reflections on how the self is similar to and different from others (1992). Ricoeur's account of the self differs from both a Hegelian or Marxist dialectic, because Ricoeur's account does not move toward an ego-centred, synthesised self. Psychologically, the dialogical process de-emphasises ego boundaries and interprets the world in conversation with others. Drawing from philosophical anthropology, Ricoeur focuses on the concept of 'reciprocity' and cites

The Golden Rule, Hillel, and the Gospels to explain how it works (1992, p.219). Reciprocity constructs the self as a moral being who depends on others. By emphasising the dependent, contingent character of the self, Ricoeur avoids constructing man as the self and woman as his permanent 'other' and encourages all persons to see themselves at times as the 'other'. Beauvoir's reflections on woman as permanent other and Ricoeur's analysis together suggest that men can be frozen into the position of the centred self. To produce a dialogical self, men will also need to see themselves as the 'other'. Men who can experience themselves as objects can become more complete subjects, and women who can experience themselves as centred selves similarly gain.

At this point it is important to understand that when I am speaking about an experience of the self as object, I am not alluding to the modern notion of a person being treated as a thing. I am building on Ricoeur's work which explains that a discourse on the self is a discourse in which the 'I' is treated as the object of investigation and reflection (1992, pp.40–55). To understand the self, one splits the self into 'I' (the investigator) and the 'self', the stilled object of investigation – the 'subject' of examination. The implication here is that there is no self-understanding without an understanding of the other because such understandings occur simultaneously. Ricoeur shows that the tension between the community and the individual is a modern dilemma that can be set aside by a different interpretation of the self.

In some regard, men are engaging in this sort of work in the current men's movement, which encourages male-bonding, self-expression, and storytelling. As men focus on themselves as the object of their inquiry, they come closer to understanding themselves in relationship to others. Thus, men are not the 'normal', regular persons, but males, which is meaningful in the context of another sort of person, a female. Once men can afford to see themselves as male, they can reflect more fully on *them*selves. This formulation of the self in relationship to the other deconstructs the abstract modern 'normal' person, which required a dual icon: male independence and female dependence. Thus, the men's movement follows the pattern of the women's movement by developing understandings of the self that depend on connections with others.

Ricoeur makes his community inclusive by constructing an interior dialogical self, whose permeable boundaries open to the world:

> To be sure, despite the affirmation of life's interiority in relation to itself, the self is essentially an opening onto the world and its relation to the world is indeed, as Brage says, a relation of total concern; *everything* concerns me. (Ricoeur, 1992, p.314.)

Although Ricoeur, Hegel, Emmanuel Levinas, and many other philosophers who talk about other-oriented constructions of the self do not include the non-human in their consideration of the other, current environmental movements, eco-feminists, and some indigenous traditions understand the self in relationship to not only humans, but animals, trees, earth, and other 'living' beings. While the feminist relational self develops from the psychological approaches used by Carol Gilligan and Nancy Chodorow, Donna Haraway expands this view to include primates, dogs, and other animal beings as co-participants in communities that extend beyond humans (Gilligan, 1982; Hallman, 1994; Zimmerman, 1994; Haraway, 1989). Robert Pirsig's tale of a relationship between a human and a motorcycle moves toward the cyborg of Haraway's dreams (Pirsig, 1974; Haraway, 1990). Native Hawaiians tell stories about the ways in which they might be brothers with sharks, the connection between the taro roots and their families, or the importance of listening to rocks to learn about life, and Lewis Thomas speaks about the connections among all cells (Buker, 1987; Thomas, 1974).

Such images expand the community of relationships to include a variety of beings: machines, plants, bikes, rocks, and animals. Shifting from a human-centric cosmology to an earth-centric one has important political implications for environmental policies and practices. Of course, this position does not require vegetarianism, since even eating plants might be understood as a violation of a human-plant relationship. But the position does call for living *with,* rather than *on,* these 'beings-objects' and constructing lives that honour these parts of 'our' selves. Therefore, this position teaches caution in destroying or mistreating 'others' because such others are part of the process of self constitution. In this story, the body is not the outer boundary of the person, but, instead, serves as a vehicle for being in the world and connecting to others. This story emphasises the self not as an abstract consciousness, but as a being that exists with other beings that have body – that have matter, which occupies space. The body matters (Butler, 1993). This anticipates a new more democratic understanding of the self which has obligations toward a variety of other 'bodily' beings.

The problem is whether this relational self can be used to develop an ethics that has moral authority or whether this self is doomed to moral relativism because relationships continually change. Can a relational self act as an ethical citizen, or will he or she just change as the culture changes? Certainly, the story of a self as the victim of cultures' whims is an apolitical position that has been well critiqued by 1990s feminism. Because responsibility depends on making the 'right' choice, ethical pluralism threatens to make choices too open. If anything goes, nothing is important. Because postmodernism avoids universal standards, it threatens to succumb to the old stereotype of the modern female, whose choices appear to be to obey cultural dictates or to rebel against all moral codes. With the disappearance of the absolutist story of universal values do postmodern selves find themselves with no ethics?

One response might be a story that goes as follows. To have moral choice and freedom, it is not necessary for a citizen to be able to choose among all possible human actions. Moral codes are ambiguous – even prohibitions on killing humans are fraught with interpretive complexities.[3] Ethics depends on a choice of at least two courses of action, one of which is better than the other; yet, what counts as 'better' is evaluated within a cultural context. Postmodernism argues that 'discovering' the one and only true value system for all persons in all times is too grandiose. But within a context, things can be made better or worse – not better in a universal sense, but better in the context of that culture. This story about moral codes avoids universal standards by placing ethical decisions in the context of historical cultural situations (Gadamer, 1976; Bauman, 1993). For the new postmodern citizen, whose ethical codes emerge in the context of relationships, the adaptable, flexible modern female offers a good starting point for reflecting on how this works.

This postmodern self reframes political relationships in three ways, each of which echoes the old modern female. First, this embodied self displaces the old story of the human whose soul makes him, or even her, master over nature and all objects with a new story of a human as a being whose life is interwoven with nature and such objects. The old master/slave relationship characterised by a subject/object tale no longer works. The new understanding implies a political shift that redefines power, refines notions of care, and displaces the psychological view of an inner self with a politicised self. Power exists in a relationship, not in a person (Sawicki, 1991). Power is gained by being with another – that other might be any participant in the cosmology of existence. Second, this new story yields a new interpretation of the phrase 'take care of yourself'. Ricoeur establishes connections between the self and care:

> The being of the self presupposes the totality of a world that is the horizon of its thinking, acting, feeling – in short, of its *care*. ... There is no world without a self who finds itself in it and acts in it; there is no self without a world that is practicable in some fashion. (Ricoeur, 1992, pp.310–11.)

Feminists have long argued that the self is relational, as can be seen in the work of Carol Gilligan, Sara Ruddick, Jean Bethke Elshtain, Patricia Hill Collins, and Nel Noddings. Elspeth Probyn explains how caring for others is connected to self-centred care: 'The care of the self thus can only be conceived of and performed within the exigency of caring for others and for and within our distinct communities.' (1993, p.169.) Ricoeur, relational feminists, and ecologists suggest that preserving the self requires becoming politically active in caring for others. From the postmodern viewpoint, 'Take care of yourself' might be interpreted to mean 'Take care of all of yourselves'. As feminists suggest, this means getting involved in politics. Third, this postmodern conception of the self augments modern ethical codes to include not only what persons do, but also what they fail to do. Ethical responsibilities expand beyond the absence of doing harm to include caring for others. Therefore, in a democratic society, poverty, racism, and sexism become everyone's responsibility. While some religious and philosophical modern traditions have already argued for an ethic of care, their arguments are based on cosmological obligations. Postmoderns reach a similar goal by reconstructing the self (Margolis, 1998, pp.86–107). In this regard, postmodernism begins with a story about the self, instead of a story about metaphysics and/or the beginnings of the cosmos, or both. It begins with the personal and moves to the political, which is a strategy proposed by second-wave radical feminists.

The postmodern self has some interesting political implications because it expects citizens to act on behalf of others. This requires decentring the self in ways that resemble the old modern female. For example, everyone has a right to call on 'my people'. However, the politics of this changes, when 'my people' have done wrong rather than simply been wronged. Forgiveness and righting wrongs become central. This also makes it hard for Euro-Americans to dismiss affirmative action arguments because 'they' did not act in racist ways. Each group, Euro-Americans, Hispanics, women, gays, the young, the elderly need to clean up their messes; 'we' did it together. The multiple, fragmented self has many ethical responsibilities. Two questions are embedded in this notion of a relational, ethical self. First, what counts as a group or community? Second, to what degree can members be responsible for each other? There are, of course, political differences between being part of an assigned class of people (female, blacks, whites, gays, the elderly) and being a part of a self-chosen community. However, the complexity in this distinction is illustrated by gay and lesbian citizens, who experience the intersection between assigned status and self-chosen political moves. Being 'in' or 'out' is a good metaphor for thinking about how all persons both are assigned to and choose group identities. The key to this is not in figuring out the essential qualities of an individual, but in figuring out how persons can live with one another.

A first step in the political ethics of living well with others is to create a context in which the self can act not so much effectively as affectionately. Ricoeur argues that humans have forgotten their 'desire to live well with and for others in just institutions' (1992, p.239). Maybe they/we can remember by thinking about the modern woman. If affection were as strong a public value as efficiency, the workplace, the home, and political life might be differently arranged so that a pragmatic self could become a caring self.

Embodying the Postmodern Self: Beyond the Material

In the postmodern narrative, existence is a linguistic event, and selves are made through symbolic moves. The text of one's life is also a communicative act and so tells a story. This metaphor of text displaces former versions of existence that stressed revamping an inner consciousness or outer physical characteristics, or both, for example, hair cuts, body shapes, and clothing choices. While the masculine self tended to emphasise consciousness transformations, stereotypical feminine selves were expected to seek physical make-overs for 'self' improvement. The collapsing of the inner/outer dimension of the modern self makes way for a postmodern self that is composed out of cultural symbols: words, images, and metaphors. Rather than focusing on the proposition, 'I think; therefore I am', postmodernism suggests, 'I speak; therefore I am'. But 'I' must speak to someone, so maybe the phrase is, 'We speak; therefore "we" are'. Rather than immortality being achieved in physical terms (even Christianity tells of the resurrection of the body), immortality comes to those who leave word records. Monuments to a self are found not in bridges, buildings, homes, and tombstones, but in letters, videos, tapes, and other recordings of rhetorical moves. While the old modern self provided a role for symbolisation, this shift from the mind/matter dichotomy to the represented self makes a political difference. Representations and words work because they belong to a communication code maintained by a community of persons. Communication presupposes others and creates the possibility for connections that go beyond material exchanges and body-to-body interactions.

Drawing on a semiotic theory of meaning in which meaning depends upon the play between oppositions and differences, postmoderns understand meaning as a network of words connected by the ways in which they are similar to and different from one another. Since the postmodern narrative blurs the distinction between an inner and outer self, speaking about 'the self' involves treating the self *as* an other – as the object of discourse. Connecting authors with others does not make them disappear, but makes them a subject of scrutiny. This move can privilege autobiographical writing, for this is the writing that attempts to construct *the* self. Because the self and others are linked in a mutually constitutive activity, all writing is autobiographical. Certainly, Maxine Hong Kingston's *Woman Warrior* illustrates the permeable boundary between the autobiographical and the fictional, as do both the essays and films of Trinh Minh-ha (Kingston, 1976; Trinh, 1989a, 1989b). But readers often point out that a written work tells as much about the author as it does about the 'subject' of its discourse. A constant postmodern subtext is the author's speaking a 'self' into being without making that author the centre of the narrative.

For example, even in writing an ethnography, which is constructed as a narrative about the other, the writer is composing a self along with this other. All writing and symbolic constructions might be considered autobiographical productions of the self – collective and individual selves. Words and symbolic representations incorporate the other into the self, and symbols represent connections among these selves, who are writer, subject, and interpreting audiences.

According to semiotics, writing depends on reading just as the self depends on others. Writers and readers are intimately connected through the text. The existence of an 'I' as writer-author depends on a reader and the existence of a speaker depends on a listener. While many philosophers are concerned that conversations require goodwill (Michelfelder and Palmer, 1989), this approach argues that some goodwill is unavoidable because the existence of a symbol-making, speaking, individual self depends on others. The self includes not only the body, but the symbols that enable that body to connect with others. If citizens are so dependent on others, then to diminish the life of one being diminishes the lives of all. When readers, auditors, or conversational partners move toward ill, they damage themselves. This is the story that semiotics tells. While secular liberalism and Marxism have told somewhat different stories, their tales depend on the distribution of material resources. Liberal and Marxist approaches urge citizens to see the distribution of resources in zero-sum terms: the more one party loses, the more the other gains, even though such terms as 'win-win' somewhat soften the tale. This makes politics focus on the distribution of material objects by giving them to one party or by generating additional objects. Semiotics recontextualises politics by focusing on the way symbols constitute the world of persons and things. Semiotics explains that communication is a mutually constitutive act. Therefore, reciprocity is as foundational for social life as the competition for resources (Ricoeur, 1992; Waterman, 1994, pp.215–32). Words work differently than things. Words do not depend on ownership and scarcity, but work because they circulate among persons. Words connect citizens in the co-operative activity of generating some common values. The story of modern woman, which emphasises connections and co-operation, suggests narratives about how fragmented multiple selves can be formed and reformed in relationship to others. The skin does not confine the body because symbolic constructions, which are manifestations of the self, flow from the body to intersect and mingle with others. In the beginning of body politics is the spoken word, which serves as a base for other types of actions.

Reflecting on the Modern Female Self: Beyond a Horizon

I have told a tale in which the fragmentary, culturally dependent postmodern self resembles the old modern feminine self, who was represented as dependent, fractured, and irrational. She is culturally produced by her associations with independent men. Although this old feminine self was not accepted as a full citizen in the modern state, postmodern politics (which include, but go beyond, states) appreciates fragmentation and cultural dependency, which offers the flexibility necessary to function in multicultural communities. Whether such communities are composed by ethnicities or variations among corporate styles, this postmodern dependent figure is encouraged to work with others and to acknowledge how he himself or she herself, as a team member, is like the others and different from them. She/he is different not so much because of an inner secret self, but because of the diverse social contexts (family, sex, class, and ethnicity) that compose that self. No longer does experience set each individual apart, because it serves as the means by which individuals develop a variety of selves. Cultural experiences are common denominators that offer a cafeteria of choices as citizens interpret experiences in order to symbolise their values. Experience is the product of cultural narratives. But those narratives are central features in the construction of coalitions, communities, and relationships. If citizens begin to tell the postmodern tale that what makes selves into citizens is their ability to act collectively, then postmodernism can recontextualise politics by bringing the old feminine values into public favour.

Thus, responsibility for actions, like power itself, is a shared phenomenon as citizens expect themselves to be a part of and care for others, including other living beings and non-living beings in their environment. The world calls citizens to care for others by acting on behalf of the multiplicity of connections that make a self. Sidestepping arguments about human nature, postmoderns reframe political issues by showing how representations and rules are themselves ambiguous. In new contexts, fixed concepts easily lose their unity and crack. Gender-bending demonstrates how sex is as much a performance as a fixed, essential quality. Persons cross-dress and in other ways recompose themselves by drawing from cultural constructs: a variety of styles, career paths, body-building techniques, cosmetics, and costumes, as well as methods of analysis, philosophical schools of thought, ideologies, and psychological habits of being. Like the modern female, postmodern selves are relational, interdependent citizens whose ethical guides develop out of commitments to others, rather than out of the application of pre-existing codes.

Care and the call to being in the world are vocations that depend on symbolic action. Because political action is not limited to the distribution of material resources, citizens need to worry as much about how they share stories and information. In fact, stories shape how food and money are distributed. Modernity's horizon focused on facts, things, fixed orders, and unified bodies. The new horizon politicises bodies, delights in fragmented lives, seeks multicultural citizens, bends gender, and scrutinises virtual realities. Perhaps the postmodern self is a version of the modern female. So, postmodern politics can look toward the modern female for some insights on what is to be done next.

NOTES

1. I use 'his' to retain the masculine imagery in the phrase.
2. This is not to argue that citizens can move from one identity to another without specialised knowledge or obligations.
3. Issues such as the use of self-defence, poverty, the cost of medical care, abortion, drug abuse, liability in automobile accidents, and smoking generate confusions about the causes of death and the responsibilities for maintaining the lives of others.

REFERENCES

Adams, C. J. ed. 1993. *Ecofeminism and the Sacred*. New York, Continuum.

Bauman, Z. 1993. *Postmodern Ethics*. Cambridge (MA), Blackwell.

Beauvoir, S. de. 1952. *The Second Sex*. trans. H. M. Parshley. New York, Knopf.

Bell, D. and Klein, R. eds. 1996. *Radically Speaking: Feminism Reclaimed*. North Melbourne, Spinifex.

Bresnahan, E. M. 1994. Responding to liberalism's 'woman problem': a feminist critique of communitarianism. Ph.D. diss., Yale University.

Buker, E. A. 1987. *Politics Through A Looking Glass: Understanding Political Cultures Through a Structuralist Interpretation of Narratives*. Westport (CT), Greenwood Press.

Butler, J. 1990. *Gender Trouble: Feminism and the Subversion of Identity*. New York, Routledge.

1993. *Bodies that Matter: On the Discursive Limits of 'Sex'*. New York, Routledge.

Collins, P. H. 1991. *Black Feminist Thought: Knowledge, Consciousness, and the Politics of Empowerment*. New York, Routledge.

Edge, H. L. 1994. *A Constructive Postmodern Perspective on Self and Community: From Atomism to Holism*. Lewiston, The Edwin Mellen Press, Ltd.

Eisenstein, Z. R. 1988. *The Female Body and the Law*. Berkeley, University of California.

Ferguson, K. E. 1993. *The Man Question: Visions of Subjectivity in Feminist Theory*. Berkeley, University of California Press.

Flax, J. 1990. *Thinking Fragments: Psychoanalysis, Feminism, and Postmodernism in the Contemporary West*. Berkeley, University of California Press.

Fuss, D. 1989. *Essentially Speaking: Feminism, Nature & Difference*. New York, Routledge.

1991. ed. *Inside/out: Lesbian Theories, Gay Theories*. New York, Routledge.

Gadamer, H-G. 1976. *Philosophical Hermeneutics*. trans. D. E. Linge. Berkeley, University of California.

Gilligan, C. 1982. *In a Different Voice: Psychological Theory and Women's Development*. Cambridge (MA), Harvard University Press.

Hallman, D. G. ed. 1994. *Ecotheology: Voices from South and North*. Maryknoll (New York), Orbis Books.

Haraway, D. 1989. *Primate Visions: Gender, Race, and Nature in the World of Modern Science*. New York, Routledge.

1990. A manifesto for cyborgs: science, technology, and socialist feminism in the 1980s. In *Feminism/Postmodernism*, ed. L. J. Nicholson, pp.190–233. New York, Routledge.

Hartsock, N. C. M. 1983. *Money, Sex and Power*. Boston, Northeastern University Press.

1990. Foucault on power: a theory for women? In *Feminism/Postmodernism*, ed. L. J. Nicholson, pp.157–75. New York, Routledge.

Hegel, G. W. F. 1977. *Phenomenology of Spirit*. trans. A. V. Miller. Oxford, Clarendon Press.

Hekman, S. 1990. *Gender and Knowledge: Elements of a Postmodern Feminism*. Boston, Northeastern University Press.

hooks, b. 1995. *Killing Rage: Ending Racism*. New York, H. Holt and Co.
Kariel, H. S. 1989. *The Desperate Politics of Postmodernism*. Amherst, University of Massachusetts Press.
Kingston, M. H. 1976. *The Woman Warrior: Memoirs of a Girlhood Among Ghosts*. New York, Knopf.
Kundera, M. 1984. *The Unbearable Lightness of Being*. trans. M. H. Heim. New York, Harper & Row.
Levine, G. ed. 1992. *Constructions of the Self*. New Brunswick (NJ), Rutgers University Press.
Margolis, D. R. 1998. *The Fabric of Self: A Theory of Ethics and Emotions*. New Haven, Yale University Press.
Michelfelder, D. P. and Palmer, R. E. 1989. *Dialogue and Deconstruction: The Gadamer-Derrida Encounter*. Albany, State University of New York Press.
Pirsig, R. 1974. *Zen and the Art of Motorcycle Maintenance*. New York, Morrow.
Probyn, E. 1993. *Sexing the Self: Gendered Positions in Cultural Studies*. New York, Routledge.
Ricoeur, P. 1992. *Oneself as Another*. trans. K. Blamey. Chicago, University of Chicago Press.
Rorty, R. 1989. *Contingency, Irony, and Solidarity*. Cambridge (NY), Cambridge University Press.
Ruddick, S. 1989. *Maternal Thinking: Toward a Politics of Peace*. New York, Ballantine Books.
Sandel, M. J. 1996. *Democracy's Discontent: America in Search of a Public Philosophy*. Cambridge (MA), Harvard University Press.
Sawicki, J. 1991. *Disciplining Foucault: Feminism, Power, and the Body*. New York, Routledge.
Sedgwick, E. K. 1990. *Epistemology of the Closet*. Berkeley, University of California Press.
Shapiro, M. J. 1981. *Language and Political Understanding: The Politics of Discursive Practices*. New Haven, Yale University Press.
1992. *Reading the Postmodern Polity: Political Theory as Textual Practice*. Minneapolis, Minnesota University Press.
Thomas, L. 1974. *The Lives of a Cell: Notes of a Biology Watcher*. New York, Viking Press.
Trinh, T. M-H. 1989a. *Woman, Native, Other: Writing Postcoloniality and Feminism*. Bloomington, Indiana University Press.
1989b. *Surname Viêt: Given Name Nam*. Film directed, written, edited, and translated by T. M-H Trinh. New York, Women Make Movies.
Tronto, J. C. 1993. *Moral Boundaries: A Political Argument for an Ethic of Care*. London, Routledge.
Waterman, B. 1994. We need not be ruled by leaders: the early town meetings. In *Taking Parts: Ingredients for Leadership, Participation and Empowerment*, ed. E. A. Buker, M. Leiserson and J. A. Rinehart, pp.215–32. Lanham (MD), University Press of America.
Zimmerman, M. 1994. *Contesting Earth's Future: Radical Ecology and Postmodernity*. Berkeley, University of California Press.

5

Feminising Race

RAJANI SUDAN

The October 1997 *Life* magazine cover dramatically announces its feature article, 'Babies Behind Bars', with words and pictures that are meant to elicit very specific emotions from its targeted audience. 'More women are in prison than ever before – and their innocent children are doing hard time too.' Such rhetoric, foregrounding the black and white photograph of a small child wandering the bleak halls of a prison house, is meant to arouse both shock and anger from the audience to which the magazine panders: the middle-class, largely white, family-oriented culture to whom such sentiments might appeal. Implicit in this rhetoric, aside from the insidious judgement being passed by morally sanctioned groups supporting 'family values' on states of innocence and guilt, is the specific moment of time to which this statement refers: 'than ever before' recreates *that* instant, *that* originary moment which serves as its referent and gives foundational weight to the 'exposé' the article promises. The fantasy of origin, the pleasing belief in a moment that one can locate as 'first', is, of course, one that is invented in the instant of its articulation.[1] Called into being, as Michel Foucault might argue, *not* from a solid, cumulatively material past, but from a *present* that conjures that past, the 'tradition' of family values, replete with originary meaning, can establish itself as a juridical body seeking to maintain ideological hegemony. The question posed by this text, then, is not about the putative guilt or innocence of mothers and their babies, but, rather, one that examines our need to depend on ideological fantasies in order to organise our lives and establish certain 'truths' we hold to be self-evident.

It seems that of the multifarious 'truths' that have been at the forefront of feminist politics ('truths' that this issue of CRISPP is devoted to problematising) the 'truth' of gender has been the most compromising. Shifting notions of 'women' have historically served as a conveniently plastic category that lock the feminine within behavioural practices whose parameters have been meted by the less visible, more powerful, and ideologically dominant masculine. This category has, in turn, functioned as an index to cultural boundaries, a way of judging or testing political perimeters. Take, for example, the ways in which contemporary Western, primarily American, culture determines the morality of sanctioned substance abuse. The cautionary label on bottles of alcohol, issued by the federal government, states *first* that 'according to the Surgeon General, women should not drink alcoholic beverages during pregnancy because of the risk of birth defects', while only secondarily does it warn that the 'consumption of alcoholic beverages impair [one's] ability to drive a car or operate machinery, and may cause health problems'. Even if we ignored the fact that the secondary warning is probably much more germane to the majority of drinkers than the first (certainly, its effects are much more widely and dramatically felt), it is curious that the use of 'women' only in their capacity of child-bearers is invoked, as if articulating the anxiety that the enormous responsibility of procreation may be relegated to the potentially careless and morally inferior bodies of women. The bodies of women, situated as barometers of public health, perform a good deal of work: they metabolise ideological structures in comfortingly visible and familiar ways.

Such uses and abuses of gender are hardly new. Economic and political health in nineteenth-century Britain, especially at the advent of the industrial revolution, depended quite heavily on the ideological positions women maintained.[2] Contemporary cultural identities thrown into flux by the social and economic discourses of postmodernism and postindustrialism, but also, perhaps more radically, by feminism, may well resonate with the ways in which modernism and industrialism destabilised nineteenth-century ideological structures.[3] Social anxieties expressed about gender in both the nineteenth and twentieth centuries privilege the importance of stabilising or solidifying gendered subjectivities into palpable 'truths' that become increasingly self-evident as they are more seamlessly naturalised and accommodated by culture, high, middle, and low.

Sites of high cultural discourse (for example, special issues of academic journals such as this one) even while they problematise identities with theoretical sophistication and postmodern finesse, may be informed by the more pedestrian anxiety to redress paradigms in terms of established boundaries: to 'know' a 'truth' in the face of a fluid postmodernism. It behoves us then to look for 'higher' articulations of identity (most insistently produced by the academy) at 'lower' sites: perhaps, as Foucault reminds us, by finding histories in the most unpromising places (1977).[4] In other words, examples of abstract theoretical paradigms of identity that are formulated in academic discourse may well be already at work in other registers, particularly ones that are the most dissociated with the academy. Foucault's injunction distinguishes 'histories' from historiography: the latter is the written testament to the former, but the very process of writing (as in any representational enterprise) is one that necessarily forecloses other phenomenological events. Like the *Life* magazine article, historiographical 'truths' are called into being in the moment of their inscription, even if they rely on an established 'history' for their articulation.

The putatively stabilised 'truth' of gender has been uncovered by feminist theory as an overdetermination. Clearly the category 'women', working overtime, has had to speak or, more accurately, *not* speak for differently situated groups.[5] Of those situations, sexuality and race have been historically marked as somehow functioning without 'women's' embrace. I would like to take up the issue of race as one that crucially situates newer formulations of 'woman'.[6] That is, as categories that harbour visibly marked bodies, gender and race have had to demonstrate the outreaches of cultural subjectivity: their bodies function as boundary creatures that describe the parameters and perimeters of social identity. Donna Haraway describes such creatures as 'odd' because of their:

> destabilizing place in the great Western evolutionary, technological, and biological narratives. [They] are, literally, *monsters*, a word that shares more than its root with the word, to *demonstrate*. Monsters signify ... The power differentiated and highly contested modes of being these monsters may be signs of possible worlds – and they are surely signs of worlds for which we are responsible. (Haraway, 1991, p.2)

But just *how* do representations of gender and race get encoded first as oddities and then as the monsters Haraway narrates? Given a popular culture that eschews 'politics' in favour of an ostensibly objective 'fashion', it would seem that the presence of boundary creatures would serve the interests of the latter category. In fact, it is the alleged objectivity of popular culture, an aggressive disinterest in the ways in which the political arena affects (or afflicts) other cultural sites or the ways in which political contestations get co-opted and neutralised as 'fashion' that renders this discursive space *excessively* political. I want to claim popular culture as a crucial discourse to understanding the shifts in feminist epistemology, from the exclusive identity of 'woman' that provided the groundwork for women's rights in the 1960s to radical disruptions of such an identity. I will not argue that such shifts are progressive; rather, I am interested in the ways that ideologies of race may generate re-articulations of gender within disturbingly familiar parameters. I am primarily concerned with the ways *new* racial categories get invented and disseminated in popular culture. For example, while constructions of race are embodied by colour (African-American, Chicana, Latina, or post-colonial third world) there are other groupings that may have remained *unmarked* by colour and are therefore in radical need of being made visible as the racial body. I will argue that the status of 'Asian' in this context is just such an example. Nancy Hartsock contends that:

> human activity has both an ontological and epistemological status ... The production of the linked processes of consciousness and material existence is directed by human attempts to satisfy physical needs, a process that leads in turn to the production of new needs ... They form for Marx a 'definite *mode of life*'. (Hartsock, 1985, pp.95–6.)

In Hartsock's and Marx's estimation, the connection between what we understand as psychic impulses (human behaviour driven by the vicissitudes of need and desire, consciously or unconsciously understood) is inextricably linked to the multifarious ways in which the vicissitudes of the marketplace take shape. In this sense, the marketplace *is* epistemology. It should come as no surprise, then, that the more reviled modes of production or cultural detritus signify as fully as the 'highest' abstract intellectualism. That is, the most lowly form of text, say, for example (in print culture) the comic book, has the same *representational* status as Kant's *Critique of Pure Reason*, not because they speak the same language, but because they are both produced out of cultures that share ideological standpoints. Popular culture not only contributes to the marketing of epistemological structures (that perhaps later get solidified in higher forms of discourse), but, in fact, constitutes epistemology. I am interested in looking at two examples of popular discourse to demonstrate the ways in which representations of race are featured as 'boundary creatures' that reflect and disrupt ideologically dominant structures about gender.

I am particularly concerned with investigating the ways these 'non-innocent monsters' simultaneously occupy positions of high visibility and invisibility, as both visibly coloured racialised bodies and as culturally seamless subversive mimics.[7] These examples are drawn from what I am naming 'middle-brow' consumerism and from 'low' culture: *The New York Times Magazine* and Barry Levinson's popular Hollywood film, *Disclosure*.[8]

I mentioned earlier that representations of 'woman' have historically marked political and economic positions in Western culture. Sally Shuttleworth's argument for popular medical advertising in mid-Victorian culture is a case in point (1990). Reading the ways in which advertising reflects the reinvention of human medical needs, Shuttleworth argues very persuasively how nineteenth-century anxieties about industrialism may have been displaced onto the model of the woman's body. The impetus the medical community had to secure the free circulation of her organs and blood (specifically of her reproductive organs of which menstrual flow was the primary barometer) in order to keep reproductive health in good working order clearly signifies other anxieties about keeping the circulation of an industrial economy in a similarly healthy, productive condition. The potential blockages to free circulation, according to this argument, figured, ironically, in part by the woman's own reluctance to manage and maintain her menstrual flow, could incur other damaging blockages that in turn might cause mental disorders (primarily hysteria). Yet, women were simultaneously figured as divorced from the material realities of the body: they were 'angels', disembodied beings that offered spiritual refreshment to family members (fathers, brothers, husbands, and sons) returning from the contaminating workplace. As these otherworldly creatures, women were situated on the outskirts of material production, even while literally being the bodies who bore the labour of reproduction.

The production of industrialism itself involved a good bit of digging around, not only medically as in the excavation of women's bodies and minds in order to formulate certain 'truths' about the hydraulics and biomechanics of gender, but literally. Digging sewers, mining, digging canals for the management of filth and the free circulation of lucre was a crucial part of constructing a competitive marketplace. It is no accident that the external manifestations of free circulation represented by all this digging is resonant with the internal workings of female reproduction: in both cases, the human invention of heavy machinery in order to furnish the means by which such digging could be accomplished is spotlighted. Little wonder, then, that despite the inflammatory controversies informing the use of the speculum (the primary gynaecological tool employed for measuring female reproductive health) it gained popularity during this same period. Such evidence points to Shuttleworth's contention that a 'strong impetus behind Victorian ideologies of womanhood' may 'spring from the problems involved in assimilating *men* to the new conditions of the labor market' (1990, p.54). Yet, while machinery enabled these signs of economic and political 'progress', the interface between man and machine was regarded with a good deal of trepidation and ambivalence even while offering a resolution of gender. Might we be able to situate our own ambivalences with changing marketplaces and technological development as the displacement of an uneasy resolution about gender and race, a resolution that is forecasted *first* in the arenas of popular discourse (not unlike nineteenth-century medical advertising) and *then* in terms of the theoretical debates of the academy?

The New York Times has long enjoyed a solid reputation in the world of journalism. Its careful slogan, 'all the news that's fit to print', dissociates the august paper from any contamination by sleazier versions of tabloid press, and implies that the paper is, in fact, a juridical institution, endowed with enough awareness of propriety to determine what constitutes 'fit' news. In fact, this is not the case, as cover stories from its Sunday *Magazine* section clearly demonstrate. Just as sensational as its less glossy counterparts, *The New York Times Magazine* capitalises on the pleasures, desires, and anxieties of a middle class that provides a form of 'middle-brow' consumption, despite its claims to a 'higher-brow' audience. The covers and issues of the *Magazine* I have chosen to examine for the purposes of this argument deploy their representations of pleasure, desire, and anxiety as raced and gendered subjectivities, that is, the faces that these pleasures and desires and anxieties assume are visibly marked by race and gender. These are the faces that the *Magazine* chooses to address the new conditions *post*industrialism, globalism, and technology impose upon the marketplace.

The magazine covers and their accompanying articles are primarily concerned with the kinds of shifts the rise of an 'Asian' economy has forced Western markets to accommodate. In 1996, the Sunday *Magazine* forecasted the beginning of the twenty-first century with a sensationalist 'exposé' of the 'New China'. Its cover featured an unsmiling and self-consciously inscrutable young Chinese man dressed at what was then the height of Parisian fashion. He is a figure very much at odds with the aesthetic our culture identifies as the grey anonymity of a post-Cultural Revolution, Maoist, Peoples Republic of China. The twenty-first century promised by the magazine's title is embodied for us most visibly in a postmodern fashion sensibility: the vogue haircut, the sunglasses, the stand-up collared navy pea-jacket, all of which are clearly Western in conception if not necessarily in manufactured origin.[9]

In a curious inversion of the ways in which global politics are conventionally represented by US media, *The New York Times Magazine* issue on China isolates and spotlights 'China' against a monolithic 'world'. The effect, however, is not to subordinate the rest of the 'world' (for example, the ways in which Western uses of the term 'Asia' erase discrete boundaries of national identity and eradicate any possibility of cultural agency those nationalities may wield), but, ironically, to *recontain* 'China' as a politically unstable, potentially socially disruptive threat to the integrity of Western (which is now synonymous with 'world') capitalist identity. The fact that the authors of this issue (Ian Buruma, Seth Faison, and Fareed Zakaria) have names that are not immediately recognisable as European only serves to solidify the ways in which a 'world' is constructed from hierarchies of Western imperialism, and that reconstruction takes shape as the 'New World Order' to contest any bid for agency on the part of 'oriental' identity.

In fact the latter scenario has been the target of a good deal of occidental anxiety. The second cover of *The New York Times Magazine* demonstrates this anxiety in very concrete ways, primarily through the excessive response to the putative demise of third-world industrial wealth.[10] Foregrounding the massive, tabloidesque typeface of the cover's text is a small replica of a globe that displays the part of the world we understand as 'Asia': the enormous land mass that includes the Asian part of the former Soviet Union, China, India, and Southeast Asia. The text reads, in descending order of size, 'Going Out of Business Sale! Asian Industries Humbled! Looking for U.S. Investors! Will Acquiesce to American-Style Capitalism! The *Real* Asian Miracle.' Underneath these alarming headlines is a smaller article titled '"Asian Value" Was Always a Myth' that is set aside in parentheses. What is one to make of this copy and this layout?

Part of the problem with reading or analysing such 'texts' is the connection between the 'actual facts' and their representation. That is, the *fact* of the collapse of the Asian market is not the phenomenon under investigation, either in this essay or, I would argue, on the cover of *The New York Times Magazine*. While the *Magazine* purports to offer an objective account of the demise of Asian markets, it is also clear by the layout of the cover that this objectivity is suspect. The cover's copy self-consciously employs tabloid strategies in order to announce the articles to which this issue is devoted. Yet this irony barely conceals the anxiety informing it: the exclamatory remarks are sustained, as it were, by the parenthetical revelation that 'Asian values' are, in fact, a *myth*. The concept of such values certainly resonates with the occidental popularity of 'family values': the article's author, Walter Russell Mead, argues that 'the financial crisis has exposed the "Asian values" of hard work, thrift and family for what they always were: bunk'. Curiously, while Mead makes half-hearted and vague acknowledgements of Western corruption, his relish is obvious in describing a case of 'Asian' depravity in very specific detail:

> For example, a recent Japanese banking scandal revolved around executives taking high-ranking officials to 'no pants' restaurants, where the waitresses don't wear underpants and the floors are made of mirrors. Now try to imagine John S. Reed taking Alan Greenspan out to a strip joint to get better treatment for Citicorp – and getting it. ... The real problem is that the very concept of Asian values is hollow. ... modern Asian history is the story of Asia's eager, wholesale adaptation of Mediterranean cultures and ideas. (Mead, 1998, p.38.)

This Asian lapse of values takes shape most dramatically as sexual debauchery, an association grounded in hundreds of years of colonialist representation of the East that mapped fantasies about sexual excess onto the edges of imperial rule. Mead's foreclosure of Asian agency, however, suggests that these fantasies may function more vociferously as markers of apprehension about the West's, and especially the USA's, unique capacity for imperial rule.[11] The fact that the devaluation of Asian economic power rests on American moral sanctions about sex that, in turn, are embodied in women's bodies (the waitresses whose only purpose in an entrepreneurial world is to mirror back tantalising glimpses of their genitalia) may reflect a cultural fear that the reproductive faculties of American economies.[12] What gender and post-colonial studies have taught is that Western representations of the foreign or exotic inevitably get displaced and conflated with the representation of the feminine. Mead's collapse of moral depravity onto the bodies of those hapless waitresses, deprived of any agency other than servitude, re-articulates for a postmodern public the need to re-establish the third world in a similar position. Divested of any kind of competing edge constructed by discourses that deconstruct ideologies of race and gender, the chastened third world ('Asian Industries Humbled! Will Acquiesce to American-Style Capitalism!') will remain a mystified entity, looking to the West for its 'values': 'Asia ... will look more and more like western Europe and North America and less and less like traditional Asia. It's called progress, and it is, despite many shortcomings, a good thing.' (Mead, 1998, p.39.) Mead thus *confirms* the threat posed by Asian corporate enterprise to American hegemony in the global marketplace. These enterprises, touting as did Lee Kuan Yew of Singapore, the *differences* Eastern values make in a competitive marketplace, have learned, according to Mead, their bitter economic lesson through a social one. 'Real' values are the sole property of Western (patriarchal) families, and, in fact, 'Asian' values of 'the extended family ... and the cultural imperatives of thrift and self-reliance' have always been Western in origin (Mead, 1998, p.39).

These readings of *The New York Times Magazine* covers may be dismissed as merely speculative, and perhaps they would be if this were the only place where such fears and fantasies got aired. When read in conjunction with other, more widely disseminated and consumed, representations of the same anxieties, however, the climate changes. Barry Levinson's *Disclosure* also articulates an unqualified celebration of middle-class familial structures, but it does so through a very complicated understanding of late capitalist enterprise, and postindustrial anxiety. The popular bugbear of public fantasies about American independence (the corporate takeover) is the bad guy in this film, but the guy turns out to be a girl. It seems, according to this film's lesson, that the most visible accomplishment feminism has taught its somewhat ungrateful daughters is to replicate the ruthlessness often attributed to men in the marketplace. In fact, feminism turns out to be responsible for the reprehensible practices (again long attributed solely to white men) of sexual harassment and racism of the kind practised by the film's female antagonist. Only the nonconformist and renegade manipulation of technology on the part of the beleaguered male protagonist in the eleventh hour, represented most visibly by his consultation with the database icon, the 'help angel', is able to uncover successfully the virulence of corporate greed, and save the company for democracy (which turns out to be a return to an idyllic hegemony). In all of the hero's travails, however, his family continues, unproblematically and even unaffectedly, to be the single source of unqualified support.

Barry Levinson's *Disclosure* warns about the dangers of sexual mismanagement, but as in Mead's example, the enthusiasm of this lesson is suspect. The sexual plot of the film, however, is secondary to the other kinds of touching that prove to be so dangerous for American business. That is, the problems of manufacture (and who controls the production line) turn out to represent deep-seated anxieties about the place for endangered white masculinity in a global economy. In fact, during one of the more dramatic scenes of the film, Tom Sanders (Michael Douglas) makes the anxiety about his race and gender quite explicit to his wife and Chinese nanny: 'Why don't I just *be* that evil white man you're all complaining about?' he shouts, 'Come on down here Chau-Minh, I want to exercise my dominance; I have a patriarchal *urge*.' The 'urge' to 'be', articulated in this context as a challenge to reclaim authority within a familial context, also clarifies the question of his corporate identity. Faced with the dissolution of his place within the Digicom Corporation during the confusion of a merger, Sanders represents the kind of maverick sensibility so dear to American ideologies of national identity.

Quite apart from the complex issues of gender and power that this film hopelessly simplifies, the more insidious concerns about race, technology, and the race for technology get cloaked, as it were, by the sexual plot. Once again, the family materialises as the redemptive unit, one that can 'save' the American economy from being swallowed by the namelessness and facelessness of 'global' politics.

What does this film in fact disclose? Tom Sanders, head of the manufacturing division of a very lucrative computer corporation, Digicom, eagerly anticipates a well-deserved promotion that will also, in his words, 'make us rich, I mean really rich'. His hopes get dashed when he is bypassed by the corporation president, Bob Garvin (Donald Sutherland), who instead brings someone else in from 'outside'. Meredith Johnson (Demi Moore), Sanders' former lover, is given the position, and it is clear that this is an unpopular choice with the company, especially because of Garvin's putative reasons for addressing gender equality in the workplace. Johnson asks Sanders to come up to her office for a drink to 'catch up', and proceeds to make sexual advances. Sanders resists and finally flees, leaving a vindictive and half-dressed Johnson screaming threats about his job after him. The rest of the film uncovers the various machinations on the part of a very clever and manipulative Johnson to remove Sanders entirely from the company and spin-off he helped create. Sanders, however, retaliates, and with the help of his supportive wife, Susan (Caroline

Goodall), and family, his lawyer, Catherine Alvarez (Roma Maffia), as well as an unknown 'friend' who turns out to be one of his female co-workers, Stephanie Kaplan (Rosemary Forsyth), finally reveals Johnson's corruption and emerges vindicated.

In some ways, this film might have been more accurately named *Foreclosure*. The subject in question (white heterosexual masculinity) is, in fact, never seriously threatened. Rather, the possibility of outside agency (agency to be successful in the corporate world, the familial world, and the first world) manifested most obviously by the womens' various plights in the film, but perhaps more insidiously by third-world manufacture and the 'Asian' bodies that produce first-world products in the third world, is utterly foreclosed. That is, even if the suspense of the plot resides in whether Sanders will be able to prove his innocence, we have already granted him an absolute and unquestionable right to power. The other characters in the film (his wife Susan, Meredith Johnson, even his lawyer, Catherine Alvarez) are less trustworthy; they are liable to make judgements about his actions that result, apparently, from problematically automatic 'feminist' ideology. But the more insistent, though virtually invisible, questionable 'characters' are the Malaysian plant workers. Under the jurisdiction of Sander's subordinates, Arthur Kahn (Michael Saskin) and Mohammed Jafar (Jesse Dizon), the Malaysian production line for highly sophisticated computer hardware comes to play a key role in the integrity of American big business.

The film opens with a free-floating 'e' that fills the entire screen. As the camera moves backward, we see the 'e' contextualised: it is an icon for an incoming electronic message, this one from Arthur Kahn at the Malaysian plant, though we hear rather than see this information through the voice of Sanders' young daughter. The scene is a 'typical' family morning (getting children dressed, eating breakfast, and preparing for a day of work) only this particular family's engagement with these rituals is erratic rather than smoothly linear: the children are fractious and the parents frazzled. All this frenetic activity is not seen, however; conversational voice-overs convey any sense of disorder. Over all the various contestations to parental requests is Sanders' voice, reminding his daughter that because he is the father, she has to obey. She immediately replies that a friend of hers does not have a father, only two mothers.

This scene does more than establish the plot conflicts ahead by projecting them onto the familial scene: it also serves to articulate the problems with a surplus of women, both in the family unit and the workplace. Most of the voices we hear are of Sanders' wife and daughter (we do not really hear much from his younger son, except a wry comment on the atypical tie Sanders is sporting that morning) and their potential for disrupting organised activity. His daughter's fretful complaints about dress and breakfast, and his wife's equally querulous requests for more help with the children (for, after all, she also works and cannot be expected to be both a successful lawyer and a flawless mother), confirm for us an unspoken understanding that Sanders keeps the family afloat in a psycho-financial equilibrium. As if to suture our ideas about feminine surfeit, we hear the notion of surplus ventriloquised by a commuting acquaintance of Sanders. In the midst of excited talk about promotions, mergers, and spin-offs, his lugubrious voice pronounces a doomsday prophecy that turns out to have altogether too great a resonance: 'I was surplused,' he says, '20 years at IBM ... you don't see it coming ... there's no longer room for you.' He then continues to vocalise the underlying anxiety about gender in the workplace: 'I used to have fun with girls. Nowadays, she probably wants your job.'

The fact that corporate language is overtly about the problems of excess and not sexism is what is of interest. The question most visibly posed in this film, however, has to do with the latter. As an audience, we are meant to believe that the workplace is threatened, first and foremost, by the advent of aggressively business-minded women who are no longer employed solely to entertain men. This anxiety extends beyond the workplace. The very fact that the film opens with a familiarly disruptive familial scene attests to the fact that the unleashed feminine operates in a number of different venues. As the model working mother, she is unnecessarily demanding, as an ungrateful daughter she is peevish, as an aggressive competitor she is ruthless, and even as an ally in the workplace she is not demonstratively concerned with the outcome for our hero – the one woman whose support would be crucial to Sander's survival has the discomfiting nickname 'stealth bomber'. Interestingly, the excessive display of problematic women in this film fronts not only for the trepidation of masculine competitiveness in an increasingly alienated marketplace, but also for the multifarious anxieties produced by imagining third-world agency, especially in the context of a first-world economy that manufactured the parameters of 'second and third worlds' in the first place.

The overdetermined places women occupy in this film do not, however, suggest that feminism has at least accomplished a diversity of female subjectivities. This putative diversity is most dramatically represented by its disruptive, obfuscating, and destructive repercussions. For example, because no one believes Sanders' story of sexual harassment, the film insinuates that although feminist politics has usefully disrupted sexual stereotypes, its militant deployment simplifies the complexities of heterosexual behaviour, reduces these simplifications even further by unilaterally claiming the moral high ground for women, and thus obfuscates the complex network of gender ideologies. The endangered heterosexual white male's case is thrown out, even by those who love him, like the proverbial baby with the bath water. He is thus left to resecure his previously uncontested position within a power structure that has historically granted him absolute agency, and he is able to perform this task under extraordinarily adverse conditions because, as the film would have us believe, he is the only character with 'innate' capacities for reason and agency.

Once again, the issue of sexuality is deferred, though sex itself is not invisible. Rather, sex in the form of sexual harassment fronts for another kind of sabotage – as 'a friend' warns in electronic clues to Sanders, the harassment is not the central 'problem' that needs to be solved. A key to that 'problem' may be heard in Johnson's address to the company. The kind of technology that Digicom is making possible, she asserts, will 'deliver' what 'religion and revolution have [only] promised ... freedom from the physical body, freedom from race and gender, from nationality and personality, from place and time ... [it will enable us] to relate to each other as pure consciousness'.[13] The utopian vision she ventriloquises ostensibly offers admirable sentiments and social goals, but what her statement in fact *articulates* is another matter entirely. Johnson's ideal for relating as 'pure' consciousnesses suggests that bodies clog the virtuous possibilities offered by electronic discourse with their attendant ideological messiness, which mostly takes shape as differences provoked and produced by race, gender, nationality, and personality. The question that never gets asked, however, is what would *count* as a pure consciousness unmarked by such boundaries?

Certainly the Malaysian bodies that produce these hard drives and the women who force their way through the company hierarchy cannot offer paradigms of 'pure' consciousness because their bodies get in the way of technological solutions. It turns out that the problem with the production line is not a problem at all, but a deliberate sabotage of Digicom's new line, Sanders' brainchild. It also turns out that Johnson has engineered this subversion in order to garner a position of power for herself. Puzzled that the American prototypes for these hard drives work unproblematically while the ones being produced on the assembly line in Kuala Lumpur do not, Sanders begins an investigation that ends in a very public expose of the political sabotage Johnson has perpetrated. Curiously, the advocate of 'pure' consciousness actively blocks its production. Meredith Johnson literally throws her body at Sanders in an effort to displace the exposure he might otherwise have noted and to create a smokescreen covering the ways in which she has ordered the clogging of machinery in the Kuala Lumpur plant.[14]

Johnson's position, however, is one that has already been foreclosed from the dominion of 'pure consciousness'. *As* a woman (and her gendered body is continually at issue throughout the film), she is incapable of achieving such a state of Cartesian utopia; her body *must* block because it is itself a block, a clog in the system. In similar fashion, the bodies of the workers in the Malaysian plant also function specifically in their capacity as marked, racialised bodies. The 'fabrication problems' get uncovered as problems with Malaysian bodies. In a peace-keeping gesture to the Malaysian government, Johnson has been responsible for negotiating the use of 'native' workers and relaxing the strict conditions under which such sophisticated technological equipment gets manufactured, which also enables her and others in her plans to benefit from the profits Sanders will lose. The workers are putting in chips by hand, 'jamming them in with their thumbs', and air conditions are 'dirty': the machinery that regulates such rarefied conditions is, in fact, not from the firm Digicom normally employs from Singapore but some local outfit.[15] In a spectacularly public exposure, Sanders is vindicated and Johnson humiliated and ousted from her undeserved office; but just what does such vindication and ousting accomplish?

At the risk of being repetitive, it seems that *Disclosure* represents a cultural anxiety to justify hegemonic foreclosure. The 'innovations' Johnson embodies (feminist advance in the corporate workplace and a new vision of technological 'freedom') are deliberately cast as either undeserved or, frankly, utterly disruptive to the smooth operations of American corporate structures. In fact, the only 'innovation' possible is entirely informed by the assimilation: the 'white male' of such recent infamy gets reinvented as a champion of the socially marginalised, and his triumph over the frustrations of groups that seek his undeserved demise can only be heralded with moral sanction, confirming the cultural stereotype that women (and minorities) are notoriously fickle and, therefore, not completely capable of assuming the kind of cultural agency conventionally enjoyed by heterosexual white masculinity.

The upheaval promised by the 'new' discursive realm of electronics *does* occur, but the parameters of that realm are drawn according to the older measures meted out by religion and revolution. Sanders' reliance on 'help angel' icons in order to negotiate the multifarious manoeuvres Johnson is perpetrating in an effort to destroy damning evidence suggests that the forces of angelic sympathy (strongly resonant of religious conviction) are on his side. Likewise, the revolutionary position Digicom finds itself in after the merger (a point marked by a significant change in language) is one that re-articulates hegemonic structures of corporate power.[16] What such repetitions demonstrate are the ways in which the rips and tears of ideological fabrics cannot remain as extant catastrophe, but must get rewoven within the structural continuity of historiography that uses Cartesian reasoning to justify hegemonic positions. Thus the tautology of technology that reproduces an angel of help, ostensibly to *guide* one through uncharted cyberspaces, but more accurately to help *chart* those spaces as 'territories', not unlike historical religious practices that invoked *super*natural beings in order to confirm ideological hierarchies. This angel's 'help', therefore, is only the kind of help that has conventionally been offered by hegemony: technology, at least as this film would have it, can only be represented by the very terms it seeks to critique.

The manufacture of hard drives in Malaysia would, therefore, prove highly disruptive to the even functioning of corporate technology; hard drives are constructed with the material effects that define borders of computational capacity and innovation, yet the very materiality of those effects render these drives peculiarly vulnerable. They are, in effect, infinitely imprintable and only able to produce what is encoded onto them. The manual labour Johnson negotiates with the Malaysian government unbeknown to anyone that matters in Digicom's corporate power structure, while appeasing the demands of the local government for recognising the interests of nationality, also 'mean voltage irregularities and complications' according to Sanders' exposé. The Malaysian government's laudable concern for championing benefits on behalf of its largely impoverished population (at least according to myths about the 'third world') from this alien enterprise is castigated. They are unable to comprehend (it would seem simply because they are 'Asian') the needs for a putative environmental purity and stability for the manufacture of products that will be, according to the film's logic, instrumental in eradicating the impediments of marked identity. What is interesting about Sanders' statement is the fact that irregularities are conscripted to Malaysian origin and the orders for such irregularities, regardless of the consequences to the future of revolutionary technology, to a woman. While these facts visibly demonstrate the ways in which the standards of scientific advance are regulated by discourses of race, imperialism, sex, and gender, they also demonstrate with equal conviction the *vulnerability* of hegemonic positions.[17]

What films such as *Disclosure* demonstrate by their repetitive ideological standpoints is a compulsion to reformulate marked signifiers that help situate a new millennium of Western history. Thus, new racial inclusions are redefined by traditional familial structures that preclude contaminating sexuality, and new marketplaces take shape within the comforting parameters of capitalist enterprise that makes sense of both virtual and global markets by using newly marked 'Asian' bodies for 'help' with their definition. In some ways I have been showing only glimpses of part of what I am identifying as a larger political problem that sustains itself not only in postindustrial Hollywood films, but in mid-nineteenth-century formulations of subjectivity, that depend on ideologies of race, gender, class, and sexuality for their articulation. 'With the increasing social division of labor,' Shuttleworth argues, Victorian England found itself faced with 'the question of sexual difference', which became the 'focus of ideological attention', and 'concern with the partitioning of economic roles [that] was displaced metonymically onto the individual body'. (1990, p.54.)

Yet though these resonances themselves provide a comforting sense of historical continuity (even if they challenge social progress), it is within the paradigm's *differences* that I want to locate my argument. That is, problems of cultural identity in a newly emerging industrial marketplace displaced themselves onto the reproductively healthy body of the mother. Regulating her gynaecological fitness psychosomatically, making sure that enervating obstructions and dangerous blockages to the flow of her menstrual cycle were effectively removed or recontained by medical or psychological discourse, metonymically confirmed the smooth functioning of a healthy industrial economy. The feminist call for birth control and sexual freedom represented an important example of 'obstruction' and 'blockage'.

Shuttleworth's argument, while focused on issues of nineteenth-century medical practices, usefully problematises the relationship between gender and the marketplace in late-twentieth-century discourse. How have similarly informed paradigms of race in conjunction with gender been rewritten within contemporary cultural signifying practices to represent the self-evident 'truth' of dominant ideologies? It may be that the re-articulation of such ideologically informed paradigms in spite of, or even within, the new discourses of identity that feminism has helped to shape may be a reaction to the radical alterations we have had to make to our understanding of the ontology of labour, not unlike the new conditions of the marketplace made way for the new understandings of gender Shuttleworth identified in mid-Victorian England.

In the late-twentieth-century *post*industrial culture of global economy, once again feminism seems to be posing dangerous threats, yet the terms have changed. The new conditions of the labour market now have to do with *multi*national *post*industrial capitalism: the exportation of high technology and its attendant anxieties about production, jobs, and even development itself moving to the third world. The hegemonic call is not for reproductive bodies, but for reformulations of the family that bypass the reproductive capacities of the mother. It seems that sexual health now operates as the clog in the system: the overly sexed body of a successful female corporate worker and the voracious economic appetites of greedy Asian enterprises economically figured as sexual depravity because they will not, in words of Russell Mead, willingly 'shift from premodern thrift to modern consumption', attests to different anxieties about the faculty of female reproduction. Finding ourselves at the brink of another century, I wonder whether increasingly problematised categories of identity (of gender, race, class, sexuality, nationality) and the 'border war' being waged by the cyborg and the 'relation between organism and machine' may provoke more than one reactionary response on the part of those whose dominant ideological positions may be threatened.

NOTES

1. Fredric Jameson argues most persuasively how the notion of a nostalgic history is, in fact, an invention of the present. He argues: 'Historicity is, in fact, neither a representation of the past nor a representation of the future (although its various forms use such representations): that is, as a relationship to the present which somehow defamiliarizes it and allows that distance from immediacy which is at length characterized as a historical perspective.' (Jameson, 1991, p.284.) In the case of the image from *Life*, the notion of family being invoked is one that has been nostalgically

attributed to the 1950s, a time far enough back in the reaches of cultural imagination from the present 1990s to be defamiliarised.

2. Even earlier in the eighteenth century, before the 1800 census, there was a widespread belief that England's population of healthy bodies capable of donating their efforts to war, depended crucially on the reproductive capacities of women. The historian Linda Colley argues: 'A cult of prolific maternity was immensely attractive to those who believed ... that Britain's population was in decline, and to those who simply wanted more live births so that the nation might better compete in terms of cannon-fodder with France. ... Encouraging women to breed, urging the benefits of maternal breast-feeding over wet-nursing, rescuing foundlings and orphans, all of these causes became increasingly attractive to British legislators, pundits, and charitable bodies in the second half of the eighteenth century, for practical as well as humanitarian reasons. ... And anxiety about keeping British women fertile, busy and contented within the domestic sphere only deepened as more and more of them appeared to be active outside of it.' (Colley, 1992, p.240.) Regulating the spheres of domesticity by focusing attention on the maternal body reflected, it would seem, the anxieties about women's capacities for citizenry in this specific instance, just as women's capacities for corporate success may be reflected in public concerns about women's bodies.
3. Fredric Jameson argues that the condition of postmodernism (a condition identified by Lyotard) is one that is characterised most succinctly by fracture of representation. Using Jameson's understanding of the term, my own use of 'postindustrialism' refers to the economic equivalent of postmodernism. No longer entirely dependent on the economic contributions of the first world, postindustrial economies may extend to other zones, most notably, the infamous 'third world'. Even if the collapse of the Asian markets has in some ways materialised dire prognostications about the incapacities of that part of the world to compete with first-world powers, the very fact that third-world markets pose a threat at all is one that attests to occidental apprehension about their own hegemonic capacities. See Nigel Harris (1996) for a specifically political and economic analysis of this point.
4. In 'Nietzsche, Genealogy, History', Foucault writes: 'it [genealogy] must record the singularity of events outside of any monotonous finality; it must seek them in the most unpromising places, in what we tend to feel is without history – in sentiments, love, conscience, instincts; it must be sensitive to their recurrence, not in order to trace the gradual curve of their evolution, but to isolate the different scenes where they engaged in different roles' (1996, p.361). Foucault argues that one of the most obfuscating problems with historiography is the fact that we assume language retains its 'originary' meaning (or, more accurately, the meaning it assumed at the specific moment of inscription). The less confining notion of 'genealogy', in his words a 'gray, meticulous, patiently documentary' practice that 'operates on a field of entangled and confused parchments ... that have been scratched over and recopied many times', accounts for cultural shifts and distortions of past and present that do not necessarily assume a *telos* or progressive narrative (Foucault, 1996, p.360).
5. When I invoke the term 'situate', I am using it in the ways that Donna Haraway has identified in 'Situated Knowledges': 'There is a premium on establishing the capacity to see from the peripheries and the depths. But here lies a serious danger of romanticizing and/or appropriating the vision of the less powerful while claiming to see from their positions. To see from below is neither easily learned nor unproblematic, even if 'we' 'naturally' inhabit the great underground terrain of subjugated knowledges. The positionings of the subjugated are not exempt from critical re-examination, decoding, deconstruction, and interpretation; that is, from both semiological and hermeneutic modes of critical enquiry. The standpoints of the subjugated are not 'innocent' positions. On the contrary, they are preferred because in

principle they are least likely to allow denial of the critical and interpretative core of all knowledge.' (Haraway, 1991, p.191.) My argument suggests that the standpoints of feminist inquiry into constructions and contestations of 'race' and 'difference' are ones whose recodings are crucially contingent on hegemonic positions within dominant feminist discourse.

6. This is not to say that the issue of race has not been taken up by feminist criticism. Barbara Christian (1985, *passim*), Valerie Smith (1990, pp.271–87), Barbara Smith (1997, pp.25–44), bell hooks (1981, 1990, *passim*), Hortense Spillers (1987b, pp.65–81), Cherrie Moraga (1987, *passim*), Gloria Anzaldua (1987, *passim*), Gayatri Spivak (1987, *passim*), Chandra Mohanty (1991, *passim*), Barbara Jean Fields (1990, pp.95–118), and others have made crucial contributions to cultural construction and contestations of race in their work. But their work on race has been predominantly devoted to the spaces that the African-American, Chicana and Latina, and the post-colonial diaspora occupy. My position, however, differs in that I am arguing that popular culture is addressing the ways in which certain third-world markets (specifically 'Asian') have remained critically unmarked (for dominant groups) by establishing and critiquing boundaries that mark the 'Asian' as a visibly different body.
7. Of course this last phrase is drawn from Homi K. Bhabha's work and is a usefully complicated paradigm that addresses the various registers of gender and race that together supplement dominant ideological frameworks. In his *The Location of Culture*, Bhabha argues for a model of 'otherness' that performs simultaneously as the visible and invisible abject body. In these capacities, then, the colonialised other's position *vis-à-vis* their imperial parent is far more powerful and dangerous than dominant ideas about others would allow. (Bhabha, 1994, *passim*.)
8. Clement Greenberg's argument concerning the relationship between 'kitsch' and 'avant-garde' may prove particularly helpful in thinking through the notions of 'middle-brow' and 'low-brow'. Greenberg contends that 'kitsch' uses the 'debased and academicized simulacra of genuine culture' for its 'raw material'. But kitsch operates on many different levels: a magazine 'like *The New Yorker*, which is fundamentally high-class kitsch for the luxury trade, converts and waters down a great deal of avant-garde material for its own uses'. While I find Greenberg's understanding of 'genuine' culture highly problematic, his point that the machinery of popular culture (kitsch) disseminates *for its own uses* the artefacts of 'high' culture is in fact a compellingly political one. (Greenberg, 1961, p.11.)
9. There is an interesting problem in the terms of manufacture; that is, products that identify the USA as a culturally discrete presence (mostly, I might add, manifested in popular cultural *objets* and *not* in 'high' cultural artefacts that have a proclivity for roaming in order to secure cultural inviolability) are produced elsewhere. The kinds of ramifications this particular phenomenon suggest reproduce, I think, the politics of a Romantic identity that capitalises on the fantasy of incorporating the exotic, inasmuch as that incorporation *confirms* the hegemonic place of imperial cultures.
10. I am not arguing about the material realities of the marketplace here; that is, I am not contending that the collapse of the Asian market did not in fact happen. My contention is that the *ways* in which this collapse was represented in the USA portends much more than strictly economic interests.
11. Ironically, in the current state of the Clinton-Lewinsky debacle, such apprehensive fantasies may have come to pass.
12. In fact, the mirroring back of genitalia, meant to be sexually titillating in this scenario, may be read in a Freudian context that is far more problematic. In 'Medusa's Head', for example, Freud discusses the ways in which apotropaia operates in conjunction with the display of castration (and, by metonymy, the female genitals) that represents both the terrifying aspect of castration (the decapitated head of Medusa that turns the

spectator stiff with terror) and the mitigation of this effect (the stiffening assures the spectator of his unmistakable possession). Read as a cultural response to the threats posed to US economic dominance by the spectre of a strong Asian economy, the waitresses reflected genitalia (like Perseus' appropriation of Medusa's head by its reflection in his shield) are the site of the horrifying sight of Asian depravity and the reassuring knowledge (albeit through hindsight) of the demise of those other economies. See Freud (1963, pp.202–203).

13. Interestingly enough, what exactly this technology is never really gets spelled out for us in the film. It is as if the *use* of the term 'technology' in this context as an abstraction can guarantee an equally abstract purity of 'consciousness'.
14. It is, perhaps, too neat a coincidence that the etymological root of 'sabotage' (from 'sabot') is figured in the form of a wooden clog.
15. I hasten to point out the radical differences between Kuala Lumpur and Singapore. The latter's renowned admittance to first-world late capitalism acts as a necessary prophylactic to the usual contaminating Malaysian touch; hence, the air conditioners furnished by the Singaporan supplier are indisputably 'clean'.
16. Interestingly, this particular shift is marked by language. Replacing the profanity ventriloquised by virtually every member of Digicom's power team, the representatives of Conley-White ask Sanders 'Can you build the darned thing or not?' This question, far from resonating hostility, pronounces the folksy image of the American maverick whose sheer technological inventiveness is rewarded with financial profit. The maverick in question, however, is revealed to *be* that 'white male' that has been under such scrutiny throughout the film.
17. I am struck by an argument Donna Haraway mentions in her interview with Constance Penley and Andrew Ross in which she mentions Aihwa Ong's *Spirits of Resistance*. Ong uncovers the ways in which the colonial status of the Malay was created by British colonists importing Javanese immigrants for subsistence food production. 'Consequently, to be native Malay was already to be the product of a colonial migration.' (1991, p.13.) Malaysian labour is, therefore, multiply outcast: not capable of the kind of reliability the Singapore firm represents because of its unstable citizenry, those Malaysian workers can only clog the system with their staining oils.

REFERENCES

Anzaldua, G. 1987. *Borderlands/La Frontera: The New Mestiza*. San Franscisco, Spinsters/Aunt Lute.

Anzaldua, G. and Moraga, C. eds. 1983. *This Bridge Called My Back: Writings by Radical Women of Color*. New York, Kitchen Table, Women of Color Press.

Bhabha, H. K. 1994. *The Location of Culture*. New York, Routledge.

Christian, B. 1985. *Black Feminist Criticism: Perspectives on Black Women Writers*. New York, Pergamon.

1987. The race for theory. *Cultural Critique*, 6, pp.51–63.

Colley, L. 1992. *Britons: Forging the Nation 1707–1837*. New Haven, Yale University Press.

Fields, B. J. 1990. Slavery, race and ideology in the United States of America. *New Left Review*, 181, pp.95–118.

Foucault, M. 1996. Nietzsche, genealogy, history. In *From Modernism to Postmodernism*, ed. L. Cahoone. Cambridge, Blackwell.

Freud, S. 1963. *Sexuality and the Psychology of Love*. New York, Macmillan.

Greenberg, C. 1961. *Art and Culture*. Boston, Beacon Press.

Haraway, D. J. 1991. *Simians, Cyborgs, and Women: The Reinvention of Nature*. New York, Routledge.

Harris, N. 1996. *The End of the Third World: Newly Industrializing Countries and the Decline of an Ideology*. London, Penguin.

Hartsock, N. C. M. 1985. *Money, Sex, and Power: Toward a Feminist Historical Materialism*. Boston, Northeastern University Press.

Hooks, B. [Gloria Watkins.] 1982. *Ain't I A Woman: Black Women and Feminism*. Boston, South End Press.

Jacobus, M., Keller, E. F. and Shuttleworth, S. eds. 1990. *Body/Politics: Women and the Discourses of Science*. New York, Routledge.

Jameson, F. 1991. *Postmodernism, or, The Cultural Logic of Late Capitalism*. Durham, Duke University Press.

Kant, I. 1990. *Critique of Pure Reason*. New York, Pantheon Books.

Mead, W. R. 1998. Asia devalued. *The New York Times Magazine*. 31 May 1998.

Mohanty, C. T., Russo, A. and Torres, L. eds. 1991. *Third World Women and the Politics of Feminism*. Bloomington and Indianapolis, Indiana University Press.

Penley, C. and Ross, A. eds. 1991. *Technoculture*. New York, Routledge.

Smith, B. 1977. Toward a black feminist criticism. *Conditions Two*, 1 (2), pp.25–44.

Smith, V. 1989. Black feminist theory and the representation of the 'other'. *Wall*, 1989, pp.38–57.

Spillers, H. 1987. Mama's baby, Papa's maybe: an American grammar book. *Diacritics*, 17(2), pp.65–81.

Spivak, G. C. 1987. *In Other Worlds: Essays in Cultural Politics*. New York and London, Methuen.

Abstracts

Identity Crises: Identity, Identity Politics, and Beyond
SUSAN HEKMAN

The author argues that the question of identity and identity politics has sidetracked feminist thought from its task of defining a new paradigm of thought. She surveys, first, the various feminist approaches to identity and, second, the theory and practice of identity politics and argues that these issues have raised intractable problems for feminist theory that none of the approaches resolves. Her conclusion is that feminist politics should not work to 'solve' these problems, but, rather, banish identity from the political realm.

Difference as an Occasion for Rights: a Feminist Rethinking of Rights, Liberalism, and Difference
NANCY J. HIRSCHMANN

This article offers a reformulation of rights that addresses and accommodates feminist concerns of difference, particularity, context, and identity. It contends that the central liberal category of rights can be recuperated to explicitly feminist ends without being caught up in the often paradoxical and self-defeating problems in which liberal feminist rights advocacy is often mired. Focusing on difference from a feminist perspective helps us to understand the historical necessity of women's exclusion from rights and how this exclusion makes the application of liberal rights to women problematic, but it also points the way to a reconfiguration of rights, as well as of central rights categories such as freedom, equality, the individual, neutrality, and universality, that allows for a fuller and more complex realisation of differences within a rights framework. Rather than viewing difference as an excuse to deny rights to particular individuals or groups, as has often been the case for women under liberalism, the author considers difference an 'occasion for rights'.

Bodies, Passions, and Citizenship

SHANE PHELAN

The current citizen status of those such as women, lesbians and gays, and racially marked 'others' cannot be understood without reference to the role of bodies and the passions in political discourse. Previous feminist work has focused on liberalism's exclusion of bodies from public notice and the subsequent exclusion of those deemed 'embodied' to be rational citizens. Here, the author examines modern republican discourse, and argue that although republicanism is more appreciative of passions in public life, this has not translated into acceptance of 'others'. Current debates about the equality of lesbians and gays, it is argued, are centrally about what sort of passions are permissible between citizens. The body's role as a trope for the political community also invites fears for bodily integrity and coherence. In contrast to those who argue for the humanising potential of the 'body politic', the author argues that this 'trope' sustains and incites fears of the dangerous other.

Is the Postmodern Self a Feminised Citizen?

ELOISE A. BUKER

This essay begins by examining how the postmodern self echoes qualities of the modern feminine self and so encounters some of the political difficulties that have faced American female citizens. Calling on feminist political theory, the essay explores three questions. First, can a fragmented culturally diverse self that displaces the unitary autonomous self be a responsible citizen with agency? Second, can a political ethic emerge from culturally dependent citizens? Third, can words and materiality mix so that borders are contingent, fuzzy, and leaky, rather than clear cut? This essay explores the politics of these questions by interrogating the postmodern self from the viewpoint of lessons learnt by modern women's experiences and current concerns in feminist theory.

Feminising Race

RAJANI SUDAN

This essay argues that the arguments marshalled in feminist studies to identify women's oppression may have foreclosed material differences between groups of women. In particular, the issue of racial difference as it is manifested in the 'Asian-American' community has been problematic. Using representations of popular culture (magazine covers and a popular Hollywood film) this essay identifies the popular cultural need to make visible the 'Asian' body as a feminised racial subject.

Notes on Contributors

Eloise A. Buker is Professor of Women's Studies /Political Science at Denison University where she directs the Women's Studies Program. Her research focuses on feminist theories and the politics of language. She is the author of 'Talking Feminist Politics: Conversations on the Law, Science and the Postmodern' (forthcoming).

Susan Hekman is a Professor in the Political Science department of the University of Texas at Arlington. She has published on the methodology of the social sciences and on feminist theory, including (as editor) a volume on feminist interpretations of Michel Foucault. Her most recent book, 'The Future of Differences', will be published shortly by Polity Press.

Nancy J. Hirschmann is Associate Professor of Government at Cornell University and a fellow at the Institute for Advanced Study in Princeton for the 1998–99 academic year. She is the author of *Rethinking Obligation: A Feminist Method for Political Theory* (Cornell University Press, 1992); co-editor with Christine Di Stefano of *Revisioning the Political: Feminist Reconstructions of Traditional Concepts in Western Political Theory* (Westview Press, 1996); and co-editor with Ulrike Liebert of *Between the Cradle and the Grave: Feminist Theoretical and Empirical Perspectives on the Social Welfare State* (Rutgers University Press, Forthcoming).

Shane Phelan is Director of Women's Studies and Associate Professor of Political Science at the University of New Mexico. She is the author of *Getting Specific: Postmodern Lesbian Politics* and *Identity Politics: Lesbian Feminism and the Limits of Community*. She is currently working on a book on queer citizenship.

Rajani Sudan is an assistant professor of English at the University of Texas at Arlington. She has published on a wide variety of topics, ranging from Samuel Johnson, Mary Wollstonecraft and Thomas de Quincey, to film, media and popular culture.

Index

Books of Related Interest

Foucault

Robert Nola, *University of Auckland (Ed)*

Michel Foucault (1926–84) was one of the most renowned of late twentieth-century social philosophers. He covered an enormous range: from sexuality to prisons; from identity to power; from knowledge to politics. The essays written for this book range over all of Foucault's work, but their main critical focus is upon objectivity, power and knowledge. The very possibility of a critical stance is a recurring theme in all of Foucault's works, and the contributors vary in the ways that they relate to his key views on truth and reason in relation to power and government.

168 pages 1998
0 7146 4915 5 cloth
0 7146 4469 2 paper
A special issue of the journal Critical Review of International Social and Political Philosophy

Pluralism and Liberal Neutrality

Richard Bellamy, *Reading University* and **Martin Hollis**, *University of East Anglia (Eds)*

Plural societies produce divided loyalties. Ties to religion, ethnicity, gender and locale pull citizens in different directions, threatening political stability and social peace. Liberals hope to avoid such conflicts by fostering agreements on a neutral set of principles and procedures.

In this book a group of internationally renowned political theorists explore the pluralist challenge to liberal neutrality. Some defend neutrality against its critics by reinterpreting its scope and character, others search for an alternative basis for liberalism in compromise, mutual recognition or perfectionism.

176 pages 1999
0 7146 4916 3 cloth
0 7146 4470 6 paper
A special issue of the journal Critical Review of International Social and Political Philosophy

FRANK CASS PUBLISHERS
Newbury House, 900 Eastern Avenue, Newbury Park, Ilford, Essex IG2 7HH
Tel: +44 (0)181 599 8866 Fax: +44 (0)181 599 0984 E-mail: info@frankcass.com
NORTH AMERICA
5804 NE Hassalo Street, Portland, OR 97213 3644, USA
Tel: 800 944 6190 Fax: 503 280 8832 E-mail cass@isbs.com
Website: www.frankcass.com